WORLD CULTURAL
HERITAGE LIBRARY

I0113295

HISTORY OF PANTOMIME

BY
R. J. BROADBENT,

Author of "STAGE WHISPERS," etc.
TO WILLIAM WADE, ESQUIRE.
This book is dedicated as a small token of the Author's esteem and regard.
R.J.B.

PUBLISHED FIRST: 1901
REPRINT 2018 ISBN: 9781433083662 1433083663

HISTORY OF PANTOMIME

CONTENTS

PREFACE.

One of the most important factors in the making of Theatrical History has been that of Pantomime, yet in many of the published works dealing with the History of the Stage it has, with the exception of a passing reference here and there, been much neglected.

It is with a view of conveying to the reading public some little, and, perhaps, new information about this ancient form of entertainment that I am tempted to issue this History of Pantomime in the hope and belief that it may not only prove interesting, but also instructive, to all lovers of the Stage.

R.J.B.

Liverpool, December, 1901.

CHAPTER I. ORIGIN OF PANTOMIME.

From the beginning of all time there has been implanted in the human breast the Dramatic instinct full of life and of vigour, and finding undoubtedly its outlet, in the early days of civilization, if not in the Dramatic Art then in the poetry of motion with that necessary and always essential concomitant of both—Pantomime. Indeed, of the Terpsichorean Art, it has been truly observed "That deprived of the imitative principle (*i.e.*, Pantomime), the strength, the mute expression, it becomes nothing but a series of cadenced steps, interesting merely as a graceful exercise." Equally so in every way does it apply to the Dramatic Art, which minus its acting, its gestures—in a word, its Pantomime—we have nothing but, to quote Hamlet, "Words, words, words."

In observing "That all the world's a stage, and the men and women merely players," Shakespeare doubtless included in the generic term "players," Pantomimists as well: Inasmuch as this, that when, and wherever a character is portrayed, or represented, be it in real life or on the stage—"Nature's looking-glass," and the world in miniature—the words that the individual or the character speaks, are accompanied with gesture and motion, or, in other words, Pantomime, when "The action is suited to the word, the word to the action."

To trace the original origin of Pantomime, or Mimicry, we must go to Nature herself where we can find this practised by her from the beginning of all time as freely, and as fully, as ever it was, or ever will be, upon the stages of our theatres. What better evidence, or instances, of this can we have than in those studies of her handiwork? as the larger species of caterpillars, when, by stretching themselves out in imitation of, and to make their foes think that they are snakes; tigers and lions choosing a background in keeping with, and in imitation of, the colours of their bodies, in order to seize their unwary prey; and for the same purpose crocodiles imitating a rotting log; the green tint of the lizard's skin for the sake of concealment; the playful imitativeness of the mocking bird; the hysterical laugh of the hyaena; the gaudy colours of tropical snakes imitated by others, besides many other examples of Mimicry, in such as butterflies of the species *Danaidae* and *Acraediae*, the *Heliconidiae* of tropical America; and hornets, wasps, ants, and bees. All this, it may be urged, is only instinct. True; but is it not also Mimicry—the Pantomime of Nature, and, though, of course, of a different kind, and for very different objects, is, nevertheless, of a kind of instinctive Pantomime or Mimicry which each and every one of us possesses in greater or lesser degrees, and as much as we do the Dramatic instinct.

The very name Pantomime itself signifies Nature as Pan was amongst the Ancients, the allegorical god of Nature, the shepherd of Arcadia, and with *Mimos*, meaning an imitator, we have, in the combination of these two words, "an imitator of Nature," and from whence we derive the origin of our word Pantomime.

Dryden says:—

"Pan taught to join with wax unequal reeds;

Pan loves the shepherds and the flocks he feeds."

"Pan," says Servius, "is a rustic god, formed in similitude of Nature, whence he is called Pan, *i.e.*, All: for he has horns in similitude of the rays of the sun and the horns of the moon; his face is as ruddy as the imitation of the aether; he has a spotted fawn skin on his breast in likeness of the stars; his lower parts are shaggy on account of the trees, shrubs, and wild beasts; he has goat's feet to denote the stability of the earth; he has a pipe of seven reeds on account of the harmony of the heavens, in which there are seven sounds; he has a crook, that is a curved staff, on account of the year, which runs back on itself *because he is the god of all Nature*."

Bernardin de St. Pierre observes of Pantomime, "That it was the first language of man; it is known to all nations; and is so natural and so expressive that the children of white parents learn it rapidly when they see it used by the negroes."

Of the Pantomimic language—a universal language and common to the whole world from time immemorial—Charles Darwin says in his "Descent of Man," that "The intellectual and social faculties of man could hardly have been inferior in any extreme degree to those now possessed by the lowest savage; otherwise primeval man could not have been so eminently successful in the struggle for life as proved by his early and wide diffusion. From the fundamental differences between certain languages some philologists have inferred that, when man first became widely diffused, he was not a speaking animal; but it may be suspected that languages, far less perfect than any now spoken, *aided by gestures*, might have been used, and yet have left no traces on subsequent and more highly-developed tongues."

With the progress of, and also as an aid to, civilization how could the traveller or the trader, not only in the beginning of time, but also now, when occasion demands, in their intercourse with foreign nations (unless, of course, they know the language) make themselves understood, or be able to trade, unless they were or are able to use that "dumb silent language"—Pantomime? Civilization undoubtedly owes much of its progress to it, and, also the world at large, to this only and always universal language. To both the deaf, as well as the dumb, its advantages have ever been apparent.

Therefore, from prehistoric times, and from the beginning of the world, we may presume to have had in some form or another, the Pantomimic Art. In the lower stages of humanity, even in our own times, there is, in all probability, a close similarity to the savagedom of mankind in the early Antediluvian period as "This is shown (says Darwin) by the pleasure which they all take in dancing, rude music, painting, tattooing, and otherwise decorating themselves—in their mutual comprehension of *gesture language*, and by the same inarticulate cries, when they are excited by various emotions." It naturally follows that even if there was only dancing, there must necessarily, as a form of entertainment, have also been Pantomime. Again, all savage tribes have a war-dance of some description, in which in fighting costume they invariably go through, in Pantomimic form, the respective movements of the Challenge, the Conflict, the Pursuit, and the Defeat, whilst other members of the tribe, both men and women, give additional stimulus to these representations by a rude form of music.

The Ostyak tribe of Northern Asia give us a specimen of the rude imitative dances of early civilization in a Pantomimic exhibition of the Chase; the gambols and habits of the wolf and other wild beasts. The Pantomimic dances of the Kamchadales are in imitation of birds, dogs, and bears; and the Damaras represent, by four of the tribe stooping down with their heads together, and uttering harsh cries, the movements of oxen, and of sheep. The Australian Bushmen Mimic the leaping of calves, the antics of the baboon, and the buzzing of swarms of bees. Primitive Pantomimic dancing is practised amongst the South Sea Islanders, and other races, and just as it was, presumably, at the beginning of the world.

Having briefly traced the origin of Pantomime, and the source of dancing, let us, in order to further amplify my subject, look at also for a moment the origin of music, in the time of prehistoric man.

From Nature also do we derive this art, as "The sighing of the wind passing over a bed of reeds is Nature's first suggestion of breath," and of music. The clapping of hands and the stamping of feet is man's first element in the making of music, which developed itself into the formation of drums, bells, and cymbals, and the evolution of the same primary principle.

It has been argued, and also ridiculously pretended, that in the Antediluvian period mankind only lived in caves with the hairy mammoth, the cave bear, the rhinoceros, and the hyaena, in a state of barbarous savagery; and that only since the Deluge have the Arts been known and cities built on this terrestrial sphere of ours. Could anything be more fallacious?

We know, from the Bible, that the first man was created about six thousand years ago, and some sixteen hundred and fifty-six years afterwards the inhabitants of the world, with the exception of Noah and his family, consisting of eight souls all told, were destroyed by the flood. Noah and his family, we can take it, were of the same race of mankind then on the earth, of the same descent and of the same flesh and blood (as we all are) of our common father and mother, Adam and Eve; yet we are not told that Noah (he was six hundred years old when he went into the Ark) and his family were savages. In the 4th chapter, 21st verse of Genesis, of Jubal-Cain, we learn that "He was the father of all such as handle the harp and organ"; and in the following verse, Tubal-Cain is described as "An instructor of every artificer in brass and iron."

We learn, also, that magnificent statues were made in Egypt some six thousand years ago; and that mention is made of a statue of King Cephren, said to have been chiselled about this period, and many learned men also affirm that letters were known to the inhabitants of the Antediluvian world. All this, however, hardly looks like the work of a barbarous race, and points to an acquaintance with the Arts, at any rate of Music and Sculpture, and that of the artificers and workers in brass and iron.

To follow, for my subject, this reasoning a little further, if there was music (which, doubtless, there was) there must also have been dancing, and, if dancing, there must, in the Antediluvian age, as a form of entertainment, have also been Pantomime. On the other hand, even supposing that man, at this period, was nothing else but a complete savage, the words of Darwin, that I have quoted on a previous page, conclusively proves, I think (on a common-sense like basis), of the existence of dancing, a rude form of music, and, of course, Pantomime at this epoch.

Ingersoll's doctrine was that "The distance from savagery to Shakespeare must be measured not by hundreds, but by millions, of years."

Finally, why, and for what reason, should the Lord God, in His all-seeing goodness and mercy, punish the inhabitants of the Antediluvian world if they were only poor unenlightened savages? Was it not because they were idolaters and worshippers of idols, "And that every imagination of the thoughts of his (man's) heart was only evil continually," as the sixth chapter and fifth verse of Genesis tells us? This then being so, we know also that in every ancient form of religion dancing was one of the acts of worship, and if dancing, there must as previously stated, have also been Pantomime.

CHAPTER II. ORIGIN OF TRAGEDY AND COMEDY

—MYTHOLOGY—THE MEANING OF THE WORD PANTOMIME—THE ORIGIN OF HARLEQUIN, COLUMBINE, CLOWN, AND PANTALOON—GRECIAN MYTHOLOGY— TRANSFORMATION SCENES—THE RISE OF GRECIAN TRAGEDY AND COMEDY—THE SATIRICAL DRAMA.

In the year 2347 B.C., in Chapter 9, verse 20, in Genesis, there occurs: "And Noah began to be a husbandman, and he planted a vineyard." This is one of the first acts that Noah did after the Deluge, and it is, as history tells us, from the rites and ceremonies in celebration of the cultivation of the vine, that we owe the origin of Tragedy and Comedy.

After the Deluge God placed His bow in the heavens as His covenant with man that the world should no more be accursed; and in the first ages of this world's history, Noah and his descendants celebrated their deliverance from the Ark, the return of the seasons, and the promise of plenty in their several religious rites and ceremonies. The children of Shem had in general Asia as their portion; Japhet had Europe; and Ham, Africa.

Soon, however, religion began to lose its purity, and it then began to degenerate very fast. Men began to repair to the tops of mountains, lonely caves and grottoes, where they thought resided their gods. To honour them they erected altars and performed their vows. Amongst the Ancients their Mythology went no further than the epoch of the Deluge, and in honour of which, and also of the Ark, they erected many temples called Aren, Theba, Argus (from whence was probably derived the Argo of the Argonauts, and the sacred ship of Osiris), Cibotus, Toleus, and Baris.

The symbol by which the Mythologists represented the Ark was an immense egg. This was supposed to have been produced by Ether and Chaos, at the bidding of Time, the one ethereal being who created the universe. By Nox (Night) the egg was hatched, which, being opened into two parts, from the upper part was formed heaven, and the lower earth.

In the sacred rites of Osiris, Isis, and the Dionysia of Bacchus, the Ark or Ship was introduced. The Dove, by many nations, in their celebrations, was looked upon as a special emblem of peace and good-will. Theba, in Egypt, was originally one of the temples dedicated to the Ark. Both priests and sooth-sayers were styled Ionah or Doves. To Dodona, in Epirus, was brought this and the first Grecian oracle all the rites and history of the Thebans. The priestesses of this temple were known in the Latin as *Columbae*. It is from this word that we derive the name Columbine, which means, in the Italian, "little dove." Homer alludes to the priestesses as doves, and that they administered to Zeuth (Noah). Nonnus speaks of Cadmus, and others of Orpheus, as introducing into Greece the rites of Dionysus or Bacchus.

The Ancients, mentions Kennedy in his work on "Mythology," have highly reverenced Noah, and designated him as Noa, Noos, Nous, Nus, Nusas, Nusus (in India), Thoth, Hermes, Mercury, Osiris, Prometheus, Deucalion, Atlas, Deus, Zeus, and Dios. Dios was one of the most ancient terms for Noah, and whence was derived Deus— Nusus compounded of Dios and Nusos, which gives us Dionysus, the Bacchus of the Greeks, and the chief god of the heathen world. Bacchus was, properly speaking, Cush (the son of Ham, and grandson of Noah), though both Dionysus and Bacchus are, by ancient writers, frequently confounded with one another.

The resting of the Ark upon Mount Baris, Minyas, the Ararat of Moses in Armenia, the dispersal of the flood, the multiplication of the families of the earth, and the migration from the plains of Shinar of the descendants of the sons of Chus or Cush (as it is sometimes written), and called Chushites or Cushites, to different parts of the world, being joined by other nations, particularly those of the descendants of Ham, one of the sons of Noah. They were the first apostates from the truth, but being great in worldly wisdom and knowledge they were thought to be, and looked upon as a superior class of beings. Ham they looked upon as a divinity, and under the name of Ammon they worshipped him as the Sun, and Chus likewise as Apollo, a name which was also bestowed by the Ancients upon Noah. The worship of the sun in all probability originated the eastern position in our churches.

Another of the ancient deities worshipped by the Ammonians was Meed, or Meet, the Cybele of the Phrygians, the nurse of Dionysus, and the Soul of the World.

Nimrod, the "mighty hunter" (who possessed the regions of Babylonia and Chaldee), and one of the sons of Cush, was the builder of that seminary of idolatory the City and Tower of Bel, and erected in honour of the god Bel, and another name for the sun. Upon the confusion of tongues when hitherto "The whole earth was of one language, and of one speech," it came to be known as Babylon, "The City of Confusion." Homer introduces Orion (Nimrod) as a giant and a hunter in the shades below, and the author of the "Pascal Chronicles" mentions that Nimrod taught the Assyrians or Babylonians to worship fire. The priests of Ammon, named Petor or Pator, used to dance round a large fire, which they affected in their dancing to describe. Probably from this the Dervish dances all over the East may be traced to this source.

Kennedy observes, of the confusion of tongues at Babel, that it was only a labial failure, so that the people could not articulate. It was not an aberration in words or language, but a failure and incapacity in labial utterance. Epiphanius says that Babel, or Babylon, was the first city built after the flood.

The Cushites were a large and numerous body, and after their dispersion from Babylon they were scattered "Abroad upon the face of the earth." They were the same people who imparted their rites and religious services into Egypt, as far as the Indus and the Ganges, and still further into Japan and China. From this event is to be discovered the fable of the flight of the Grecian god Bacchus, the fabulous wanderings of Osiris, and the same god under another name, of the Egyptians. Wherever Dionysus, Osiris, or Bacchus went, the Ancients say that he taught the cultivation of the soil, and the planting of the vine. Dionysus, Bacchus, or Osiris, as I have shown in a preceding page, were only other designations for Noah.

Of the Hindu heathen deity, Vishnu, Father Boushet mentions an Indian tradition, concerning a flood which covered the whole earth, when Vishnu made a raft, and, being turned into a fish, steered it with his tail. Vishnu, like Dagon, was represented under the figure of a man and fish.

Strangely enough, the regions said to have been traversed by Dionysus, Osiris, or Bacchus were, at different times, passed through by the posterity of Ham, and in many of them they took up their residence. In his journeyings the chief attendants of Osiris, or Bacchus, were Pan, Anabis, Macedo, the Muses, the Satyrs, and Bacchic women were all in his retinue. The people of India claim him as their own, and maintain that he was born at Nusa in their country. Arrian speaks of the Nuseans as being the attendants of Dionysus. In all traditions Dionysus appears as the representative of some power of Nature.

The first who reduced Mythology to a kind of system were, in all probability, the Egyptians. Egypt was ever the land of graven images, and under the veil of Allegory and Mythology the priests concealed religion from the eyes of the vulgar. In the beginning, brute animals and certain vegetables were represented as the visible symbols of the deities to which they were consecrated. Hence Jupiter Ammon was represented under the figure of a Ram; Apis under a Cow; Osiris of a Bull; Mercury or Thol of an Ibis; Diana or Babastis of a Cat; and Pan of a Goat. From these sources are derived the fabulous transformation of the gods celebrated in Egyptian Mythology, and afterwards imported into Greece and Italy to serve as the subjects of the Grecian and Roman Pantomimes.

Pantomime as we now know the term, means, not only the Art of acting in dumb show, but also that of a spectacle or Christmas entertainment. (I may add in parenthesis, that in the early part of the last century—the nineteenth—the dictionaries only refer to Pantomime as meaning the former of the above two definitions, and not the latter.)

Pan, regarded as the symbol of the universe, was also the god of flocks, pastures, and shepherds in classic Mythology, and the guardian of bees, hunting and fishing in his Kingdom of Arcadia. His form, like the Satyrs, both supposed to have been the offsprings of Mercury, was that of a man combined with a goat, having horns and feet like the latter animal.

Mimos (Gr.), as I have stated in the beginning, means an "imitator," or a "mimic," and from which word we have the derivation of the words "mimicry," "mimetic," and the like.

Pan was the traditional inventor of the Pandean pipes, and also from his name we derive many words that are in our language, such as "panic" (Pan used to delight in suddenly surprising the shepherds whilst tending their flocks), and the other attributes of this noun, including that recently coined term of the Americans, "panicy."

Pan is said to have been the son of Mercury, or even Mercury himself, and others say that he was the son of Zeus. Mercury and Zeus, it will be remembered in Mythology, were only names for Noah. Pan is unnoticed by Homer.

A heathen deity of Italy, Lupercus, the guardian of their flocks and pastures, has also been identified with Pan, and in whose honour annual rural festivals, known as Lupercalia, were observed.

The Lupercalian festivals were held on the 15th of the Kalends of March. The priests, Luperci, used to dance naked through the streets as part of the ceremonies attached to the festival.

Mention has been made by Dr. Clarke, in his "Travels," Vol. IV., that Harlequin is the god Mercury, with his short sword *herpe*, or his rod, the *caduceus* (which has been likened to the sceptre of Judah), to render himself invisible, and to transport himself from one end of the earth to the other, and that the covering on his head, the winged cap, was the *petasus*. Apropos of this, the following lines in the tenth Ode, of the first book of Horace, will probably occur to the reader:

"Mercury! Atlas' smooth-tongued boy, whose will

First trained to speed our wildest earliest race,

And gave their rough hewn forms with supple skill

The gymnast's grace.

"'Tis thine the unbodied spirits of the blessed,

To guide to bliss, and with thy *golden rod*

To rule the shades; above, below, caressed

By every god."

Mercury, as we have seen, was among the Ancients, only another name for Noah. "Indeed," says Dr. Clarke, "some of the representations of Mercury upon ancient vases are actually taken from the scenic exhibitions of the Grecian theatre; and that these exhibitions were also the prototypes whereon D'Hancarville shows Mercury, Momus, and Psyche delineated as we see Harlequin, Columbine, and Clown on our stages. The old man (Pantaloon), is Charon (the ferryman of hell). The Clown is Momus, the buffoon of heaven, the god of raillery and wit, and whose large gaping mouth is in imitation of the ancient masks."

Amongst the Aryans, Medians, Egyptians, Chaldeans, Babylonians, and other nations (including our own, as did not Lilly predict the execution of Charles I., the plague, the great fire of London, and other events) was astrology practised. The Egyptians peopled the constellation of the Zodiac (the first open book for mankind to read), with Genii, and one of the twelve Zodiacal signs was Aries (the Ram). The ram is of the same species as the goat, and the god Pan was the Goat god, as we know. The astrologers, in their divinations and rulings of the planets placed the various parts of the body under a planetary influence. The head and face were assigned to the house of Aries, and therefore the face notably for the Pantomimic Art was placed by the ancient astrologers under the influence of this particular planet.

The heathen worship of Pan was not only known in Arcadia, but also throughout Greece, although it did not reach Athens until after Marathon.

Of Pan's death Plutarch tells the story that in the reign of Tiberius, one Thamus, a pilot, visiting the islands of Paxae, was told of this god's death. When he reached Palodes he told the news, whereupon loud and great lamentations were heard, as of Nature herself expressing her grief. The epoch of the story coincides with the enactment of that grim, and the world's greatest tragedy on the hill of Golgotha, and the end, and the beginning of a new world. Rabelais, Milton, Schiller, and also Mrs. Browning, have allusions to this story of Plutarch's.

The ambitious family of the Titans (the bones of the "giants on the earth" before the Deluge, gave rise to the stories of the Titans found in caves), and their scions and coadjutors Jupiter, Juno, Mars, Mercury, Apollo, Diana, Bacchus, Minerva, or Pallas, Ceres, Proserpine, Pluto, and Neptune furnish by far the greatest part of the Mythology of Greece. Tradition says that they left Phoenicia about the time of Moses to settle in Crete, and from thence they made their way into Greece, which was supposed at that time to be inhabited by a race of savages. The arts and inventions were communicated to the natives, and the blessings of civilization in process of time inspired the inhabitants with admiration. They, therefore, relinquished worshipping the luminary and heavenly bodies, and transferred their devotion to their benefactors. Then into existence sprang the most inconsistent and irreconcilable fictions. The deified mortals, with their foibles and frailities, were transmitted to posterity in the most glorious manner possible, and hence accordingly, in both the Odyssey and the Iliad of Homer, we have a strange and heterogeneous mixture of what is not only mighty in heroes, but also that which is equally mean.

In the Grecian Mythology the labours of Hercules, the expedition of Osiris, the wanderings and transformation of Io, the fable of the conflagration of Phaeton, the rage of Proserpine, the wanderings of Ceres, the Eleusinian Mysteries, the Orgia, or sacred rites of Bacchus, in fine, the ground work of Grecian Mythology is to be traced to the East, from where also all our nursery tales, and also our popular Pantomime subjects; (which is the subject of another chapter) perhaps, with the exception of our own "Robinson Crusoe," originated.

The nine Muses called Pierides in Grecian Mythology were the daughters of Jupiter and Mnemosyne (Memory), supposed to preside over the liberal Arts and the sciences. They were Calliope (Heroic Poetry), Clio Euterpe (Music), Erato (Love Poetry), Melpomene (Tragedy), Polyhymnia (Muse of Singing and Rhetoric), Terpsichore (Dancing), Thalia (Comedy), and Urania (Astronomy). Mount Parnassus, Mount Helicon, and the fountains of Castalia and Aganippe were the sacred places of the Muses.

The Eleusinian Mysteries are of a period that may be likened to the 7th century B.C., and at these Mysteries as many as 30,000 persons, in the time of Herodotus, assembled to witness them. The attributes of these Grecian Mysteries, like those of the Egyptians, consisted of processions, sacrificial offerings, purifications, dances, and all that the Mimetic and the other Arts could convey; add to this the various coloured lights, and the fairy-like grandeur of the whole, we have something that may be likened to the

Transformation, and other fairy-like scenes of English Pantomimes and Extravaganzas.

At the Orgia, or sacred rites of Bacchus, the customary sacrifice to be offered, because it fed on vines, was the goat. The vine, ivy, laurel, asphodel, the dolphin, lynx, tiger, and ass were all sacred to Bacchus. The acceptable sacrifice to Venus was a dove; Jupiter, a bull; an ox of five years old, ram or boar pig to Neptune; and Diana, a stag. At the inception of the Bacchanalian festivals in Greece, the tragic song of the Goat, a sacred hymn was sung, and from which rude beginning sprang the Tragedy and Comedy of Greece. The Greeks place every event as happening in their country, and it is not surprising that they claim for themselves the inception of Tragedy and Comedy, which they undoubtedly were the originators of in Greece, but the religious festivals of Dionysus, Osiris, and Bacchus, to which we are supposed to owe the inception of Tragedy and Comedy, were known long before the Greeks knew them. (Dionysus was the patron and protector of theatres.) "The purport of the song was that Bacchus imparted his secret of the cultivation of vines to a petty prince in Attica, named Icarius, who happened one day to espy a goat brouzing upon his plantations, immediately seized, and offered it up as a sacrifice to his divine benefactor; the peasants assembled round their master, assisted in the ceremony, and expressed their joy and gratitude in music, songs, dances, and Pantomime on the occasion; the sacrifice grew into a festival, and the festival into an annual solemnity, attended most probably every year with additional circumstances, when the countrymen flocked together in crowds, and sang in rustic strains the praises of their favourite deity."

Amongst the reported followers of these Bacchanalian festivals were those fabulous race of grotesque sylvan beings, previously referred to, known as the Satyrs. They were of a sturdy frame, in features they had broad snub noses, and appeared in rough skins of animals with large and Roman Mythology, the dark and more sombre legends of the Scandinavian and the Teuton; and all derived from the various names grouped round the Sun god, which in the lighter themes the Aryans associated with the rising and the setting of the sun, in all its heavenly glory, and with the sombre legends the coming of the winter, and marking the difference between lightness and darkness.

In India the origin of dramatic entertainments has been attributed to the sage Bharata (meaning an actor), who received, it is said, a communication from the god Brahma to introduce them, as the latter had received his knowledge of them from the Vedas. Bharata was also said to be the "Father of dramatic criticism." Pantomimic scenes derived from the heathen Mythology of Vishnu—a collection of poems and hymns on the Aryan religion—are even now in India occasionally enacted by the Jatras of the Bengalis and the Rasas of the provinces in the west, and, just as their forefathers did ages and ages ago. An episode from the history of the god Vishnu, in relation to his marriage with Laxmi, was a favourite subject for the early Indian Drama. Of Vedic Mythology Professor Max Müller observes that in it "There are no genealogies, no settled marriages between gods and goddesses. The father is sometimes the son, the brother, the husband, and she who in one hymn is the mother, is in another the wife. As the conceptions of the poet vary so varies the nature of these gods."

The Hindoo dramatic writer, Babhavñti—the Indian Shakespeare—introduced with success in one of his dramas, like in our "Hamlet," "a play within a play," and much in a similar way as our early dramatists used in their plays, the "dumb shows."

Between the native Tragedy and Comedy, as in China, there was no definite distinction, and, although both contained some of the best and noblest sentiments, yet the racial philosophy of caste enters greatly into the construction of each.

In the Hindoo Mythology we have prototypes of the gods of the Egyptian, Grecian, and Roman Mythologies. The god Vishnu, who, in Aryan Mythology, is the wind and "Traverses the heavens in three strides," is the greatest of all heathen deities. His dwelling-place was "The aerial mountains, where the many horned and swiftly moving cattle abide." In Grecian Mythology Hermes or Mercury took on some of the characteristics of Vishnu.

In the Eleusinian Mysteries of the Greeks, the signs and symbols that marked the worship of Vishnu by the Aryans, are apparent; and in the British Museum the scenes of the vases of the Hamilton collection agree closely with the Sacti rites of Hindustan.

After having briefly noticed and introduced Vishnu or Hermes to the notice of the reader, we will now take another of the Aryan deities—See-Va, the Wine god. This myth was the Dionysus, or Bacchus, of the Greeks, and the expedition of this "immortal" through the world to instruct mankind in agriculture, is likened as well as the god himself by the Egyptians to their deity Osiris—the god of the Nile. The worship of See-Va, Bacchus, or Osiris extended over Asia Minor, Greece, and Italy.

The visit and advent of the Wine or Pleasure god Bacchus to India, with his accompanying train of sylvan and rural deities, and nymphs, is supposed to have conquered the Hindoos, and taught them civilization, besides the cultivation of the vine. Strange to relate that when Alexander and his army reached the present Cabul they found ivy and wild vines (both sacred to Bacchus) growing in abundance, and they were met by processions dressed in parti-coloured dresses, playing on drums like the Bacchic festivals of Greece and Lower Asia of that time.

Female parts were acted by women, but it was not a general custom; and the Clown of the piece was always a Brahma, or if not, at any rate a pupil of Brahma.

Also among the minor characters was the *Vita*, "the accomplished companion," a part sometimes played by men and sometimes by women. Probably in this in the latter instance we have the origin of the Columbine and Soubrette part in after years of the European stage as the term "accomplished companion," would equally apply to both. It is only a surmise, yet history as we know is continually repeating itself—even in Soubrette parts, and in more senses than one.

Of scenic displays that it possessed there was little or none, though the exits and entrances to the stage had probably some device to denote them. What they possessed in the way of properties it is more than useless to speculate, as, whatever could be said, could only be conjectural. In dressing their parts propriety in costume, and in adhering to the habits of the Indian Drama, seems to have been observed with some show of consistency.

The Chinese Drama also arose from the Hindoo developing itself as time rolled on from Pantomimes and ballets. A very ancient Pantomime is said to have been symbolical of the conquest of China by Wou Wang. Others were on subjects of the Harvest, War, and Peace; whilst many were only of an obscure nature. With the rise and progress of the native drama about five hundred years before Christ Pantomimes fell into disrepute.

It is interesting to note that one of the penal codes of the Celestial Empire was, that those who wrote plays with vicious, or immoral tendencies, should stay in "purgatory" as long as their plays were performed. This precept was all right in theory, but in practice it was more honoured in the breach than in the observance, as amongst the whole of the Celestial dramatic writers only one in about ten thousand seems to have conformed to this rule.

The dramatic writers of China duly observed the question of rank and priority, and just as much as the native Hindoo writers observed that of the various phases of caste.

Plays were divided into acts and scenes, and occasionally were prefixed by a prologue. Performances took sometimes a single day, and favourite plays oftentimes longer.

The Japanese type of drama seems to have originally evolved itself from that of the Chinese, though its singing, dancing, historical, and Pantomimical displays are, of course, purely native.

A native of Japan, though of Chinese descent, Hadu Kawatsa, at the close of the 6th century (A.D.) gave dramatic entertainments in Japan. The Japanese claim for the Pantomimical dance Sambâso as a preventative of earthquakes and volcanic eruptions; and this dance, it is said, that within recent years, is used as a prelude to dramatic entertainments.

Isono Zenji is thought to have been the originator of the Japanese Drama, but her performances were more those of the *Mima*—dancing and posturing.

In the seventeenth century Saruwaka Kanzaburô introduced the drama proper into Japan by the erection, in 1624, of a theatre, and nearly fifty years later than the first permanent theatre that was erected (1576) in England.

Popular historical subjects were chosen for the plays, though the names of the characters were transformed. Fancy plays, operas, ballets, which in the latter women appeared, became also very popular.

Within sight of the closing years of the last century (the nineteenth), Japanese actors were more or less under a ban when the same was happily removed.

the Terpsichorean Art, Professor Desrat says, "That the Greeks, a nation of heroes, trained themselves in the art of hand-to-hand combat."

"Dancing," says another writer, "and imitative acting in the lower stages of civilization are identical, and in the sacred dances of ancient Greece we may trace the whole Dramatic Art of the modern world. The Spartans practised dancing as a gymnastic exercise, and made it compulsory upon all children from the age of five."

And we are also told that religious processions went with song and dance (and, of course, Pantomime), to the Egyptian temples; the Cretan chorus sang hymns to the Greek gods; David danced in procession before the Ark of the Covenant; and that we are to "Praise the Lord with the sound of the trumpet, praise Him with the psaltery and the harp; praise Him with the timbrel and the *dance*."

Aristotle speaks of Mimetic dances three hundred years before the Augustan era. He also says that dancers want neither poetry or music, as by the assistance of measure and cadence only they can imitate human manners, actions, and passions.

Again, "Homer, describing the employment of the Delian priestesses, or Nuns, of the order of St. Apollo of Delos, that they were great adepts in the Art of Mimicry, and that part of the entertainment which they afforded to the numerous people of different nations; who formed their congregations was, as the poet expresses it, from their *being skilled to imitate the voices and the pulsation or measure of all nations, and so exactly was their song adapted that every man would think he himself was singing.*"

Homer also mentions a dance invented for Ariadne. In the midst of the dancers, there were two dancers who sang the adventures of Daedalus, supplementing their singing by gestures, and explaining in Pantomime the subject of the whole performance.

The Pyrrhic dance of the Greeks was a sort of military Pantomime. The Greeks had several kinds of Pyrrhic dances, the names of which varied with the character of the performance.

The Hyplomachia imitated a fight with shields.

The Skiamachia was a battle with shadows,

The Monomachia was an imitation of single combat.

Some of the Mimetic dances common to both Greeks and Romans were The Loves of Adonis and Venus, the Exploits of Ajax, the Adventures of Apollo, the Rape of Ganymede, the Loves of Jupiter and Danae, the Birth of Jupiter, Hector, the Rape of Europa, the Labours of Hercules, Hercules Mad, the Graces, Saturn devouring his Children, the Cybele in honour of Cybele, the Cyclops, the Sorrows of Niobe, the Tragic End of Semele, the Wars of the Titans, the Judgment of Paris, Daphne pursued by Apollo, the Bucolic Dance, and the Dance of Flowers.

CHAPTER V. THESPIS

—THE PROGRESS OF TRAGEDY AND COMEDY— AESCHYLUS—THE EPOPÉE—HOMER—SOPHOCLES— EURIPIDES—GRECIAN MIMES—THE FIRST ATHENIAN THEATRE—SCENERY AND EFFECTS.

When Thespis first pointed out the tragic path, and when (as Horace tells us in his Odes) that "The inventor of the Art carried his vagrant players on a cart," by his introduction of a new personage, who relieved the chorus, or troop of singers, by reciting some part of a well-known history, or fable, which gave time for the chorus to rest. All that the actors repeated between the songs of the chorus was called an episode, or additional part, consisting often of different adventures, which had no connexion with each other. Thus Pantomime, the song, and the dance, which were at first the only performances, became gradually and insensibly a necessary and ornamental part of the drama.

From this time, the actor, or reciter, was more attended to than the chorus; however, his part was executed, and it had the powerful charms of novelty to recommend it, and quickly obscured the lustre of the chorus, whose songs were now of a different nature, insomuch that the original subject of them, the praise of Bacchus, was by degrees either slightly mentioned, or totally passed over and forgotten; the priests, who we may suppose for a long time presided over the whole, were alarmed at so open a contempt of the deity, and unanimously exclaimed, that this was nothing to Bacchus; the contempt grew into a kind of proverbial saying, and as such is handed down to us.

From the origin of Tragedy and Comedy, and to the days of Thespis, and from this time to that of Aeschylus, all is doubt, conjecture, and obscurity; neither Aristotle, nor any other ancient writer, gives us the least insight into the state and progress of the Greek Drama; the names of a few, and but a few, tragedians, during this dark period, are handed down to us; such were Epigenes, the Sicyonion, and Pratinas, who wrote fifty-two plays, thirty-two of which are said to be satirical. After Thespis, came his scholar Phrynicus, who wrote nine tragedies; for one of which, we are told, he was fined fifty drachmas, because he had made it (an odd reason) too deep, and too affecting; there was another, also named Phrynicus, author of two tragedies: to these must be added Alcaeus, Phormus, and Choeritas, together with Cephisodorus, an Athenian, who wrote the "Amazon," and Apollophanes, supposed to have been the author of a tragedy named "Daulis," though Suidas is of another opinion. Tragedy had, during the lives of these writers, probably made but a slow progress, and received but very little culture and improvement; when at length the great

Aeschylus arose, who, from this rude and undigested chaos, created as it were a new world in the system of letters.

Poets, and perhaps epic poets, there might have been before Homer (the latter, who, in all probability, lived within fifty years of the Fall of Troy—1250 B.C.). Dramatic writers there certainly were before Aeschylus the former notwithstanding, we may, with the utmost propriety, style the inventor and father of heroic poetry, and the latter of the ancient drama, which, before his time, does not appear to have had any particular form but that of Pantomime, song, and the union of song and dance. *Aeschylus first introduced dialogue*, that most essential part of tragedy, and by the addition of the second personage, threw the whole fable into action, and restored the chorus to its ancient dignity.

Aeschylus having, like a tender parent, endowed his darling child with every mental accomplishment, seemed resolved that no external ornaments should be wanting to render her universally amiable; he clothed her, therefore, in the most splendid habit, and bestowed upon her everything that Art could produce, to heighten and improve her charms. Aeschylus, who being himself author, actor, and manager, took upon him the whole conduct of the drama, and did not neglect any part of it; he improved the scenery and decorations, brought his actors into a well constructed theatre, raised his heroes on the *cothurnus*, or buskin, invented the masks, and introduced splendid habits with long trains, that gave an air of majesty and dignity to the performers.

From the time when Tragedy began to assume a regular form, we find her closely following the steps of epic poetry; all the parts of *epopée*, or heroic poem, may be traced in tragedy, though, as Aristotle observes, all the parts of tragedy are not to be found in the *epopée*; whence the partisans of the stage with some reason conclude, that perfection in the former is more difficult to be attained than in the latter. Without entering into a dispute, we may venture, however, to say that from Homer the tragedians drew the plan, construction, and conduct of their fables, and not unfrequently, the fable itself; to him they applied for propriety of manners, character, sentiment, and diction.

From this era then, we are to consider Tragedy as an elegant and noble structure, built according to the rules of art, symmetry, and proportion; whose every part was in itself fair, firm, and compact—and at the same time contributed to the beauty, utility, and duration of the whole edifice.

Sophocles and Euripides carefully studied the plan laid down by Aeschylus, and by their superior genius and judgment, improved it in a short time to its highest state of perfection, from which it gradually declined to the rise of the Roman Drama.

Aeschylus, Sophocles, and Euripides were the three great tragic poets; and from the works of these three illustrious writers, and from them alone, we must draw all our knowledge of the ancient Greek Tragedy.

Comedy, like Tragedy, owes its origin to the union of music, song, dance, and Pantomime; Tragedy to the dithyrambick, and Comedy to the phallica; and each of them (emulating Pantomime), began to form themselves into dramatic imitations; each studied to adopt a measure suited to their purpose:—Tragedy, the more lofty, chose the tetrameter; and comedy, which aimed at familiarity, the iambic. But, as the style of tragedy improved, Nature herself, says Aristotle, directed the writers to abandon the capering tetrameter, and to embrace that measure which was most accommodated to the purposes of dialogue; whence the iambic became the common measure of both Tragedy and Comedy.

Sophocles brought on a third actor, which number was not exceeded in the Greek tragedies during the same scene. Horace alludes to this, "*nec quarta loqui persona laboret,*" (Let not a fourth person strive to speak): but it was not observed in comedy. Players of second parts were obliged to speak so low as not to drown the voice of the chief actor. Tyrants were always played by subalterns. The women were only dancers (and Pantomimists). Female parts were performed by eunuchs.

On the Grecian stage, those performers who devoted themselves entirely to the Art of Miming originally came from Sicily and southern Italy, though the exact period is difficult to determine with any degree of certainty.

The figures of tragic or comic actors were known by the long and strait sleeves which they wore. The servants in comedy, below the dress with strait sleeves, had a short cassock with half-sleeves. That the characters might be distinguished (a difficulty in this respect arising from the size of the theatres) parasites carried a short truncheon; the rural deities, shepherds, and peasants, the crook; heralds and ambassadors, the *caduceus*; kings, a long, straight sceptre; heroes, a club, etc. The tunic of tragic actors descended to the heels, and was called *palla*. They generally carried a long staff or an erect sceptre. They who represented old men, leaned upon a long and crooked staff.

The first Greek theatre at Athens (says Fosbroke, in his "Antiquities,") was a temporary structure of boards, removed after the performances were closed. This fashion continued till the erection of the theatre of Bacchus, at Athens, which served as a model for the others. The Greek theatre was no more than a concave sweep, scooped out of the hollow side of a hill, generally facing the sea. The sweep was filled with seats, rising above each other, and ascended by staircases, placed like the *radii* of a circle. This semi-circular form was adopted not merely for convenience of vision, but for an aid to the sound. This range for spectators was called the *coilon* or hollow. The area below was the *conistra*, or pit. There was no superstructure for a gallery, but around the rim of the building were porticos, by which the spectators entered, and whither they could retire, if it rained. The portico just about the highest corridor, or lobby, was denominated the *cercys*, and used by the women. Where is now the orchestra, was a platform, called by that name; and here, among the Greeks, were stationed the musicians; chorus and Mimes; among the Romans, the Emperor, Senate, and other persons of quality. Seven feet above the orchestra, and eleven above the *conistra*, or pit, was the front stage, or proscenium, upon which stood an altar to Apollo. Here the principal actors performed, and the site of the altar was devoted to the dances (of the Mimes) and songs of the chorus. The part called the *scena* was in line with the ornamental columns, upon the sides of the stage.

The ancient scenery at first consisted of mere boughs, but afterwards of tapestry, not painted canvas. The Greek stage consisted of three parts, the *scena*, across the theatre, upon the line of the curtain in our theatres; the proscenium, where the actors performed; and the post-scenium, the part behind the house, before-mentioned. To form parts of the scenes there were prisms of framework, turning upon pivots, upon each face of which was strained a distinct picture, one for tragedy, consisting of large buildings, with columns, statues, and other corresponding ornaments; a second face, with houses, windows, and balconies, for comedy; a third applied to farce, with cottages, grottoes, and rural scenes. There were the *scenae versatiles* of Servius. Besides these, there were *scenae ductiles*, which drew backwards and forwards, and opened a view of the house, which was built upon the stage, and contained apartments for machinery, or retirement for the actors. As to the patterns of the scenes, in comedy, the most considerable building was in the centre; that on the right side was a little less elevated, and that on the left generally represented an inn. In the satirical pieces they had always a cave in the middle, a wretched cabin on the right, and on the left an old ruined temple, or some landscape. In these representations perspective was observed for Vitruvius remarks (C. 8) that the rules of it were invented and practised from the time of Aeschylus, by a painter named Agararchus, who has even left a treatise upon it. After the downfall of the Roman Empire, these decorations of the stage were neglected, till Peruzzi, a Siennese, who died in 1536, revived them.

There were three entries in front, and two on the sides; the middle entry (termed the Royal door) was always that of the principal actor; thus, in tragedy, it was commonly the gate of a palace. Those on the right and left were destined to the second-part players, and the two others, on the sides, one to people from the country, the other to those from the harbour, or any public place.

Pollux informs us, that there were trap-doors for ghosts, furies, and the infernal deities. Some under the doors, on one side, introduced the rural deities, and on the other the marine. The ascents or descents were managed by cords, wheels, and counter-weights. Of these machines none were more common than those which descended from heaven in the end of the play, in which the gods came to extricate the poet in the *denouement*. The kinds were chiefly three; some conveyed the performer across the theatre in the air; by others, the gods descended on the stage; and a third contrivance, elevated, or supported in the air, persons who seemed to fly, from which accidents often happened. (It is from this that the well-known phrase "*Deus ex machina*" has its origin.) As the ancient theatres were larger than ours, and unroofed, there was no wheel-work aloft, but the performer was elevated by a sort of crane, of which the beam was above the stage; and turning upon itself, whilst the counter-weight made the actor descend or ascend, caused him to describe curves, jointly composed of the circular motion of the crane, and the vertical ascent. The *anapesmata* were cords for the sudden appearance of furies, when fastened to the lowest steps; and to the ascension of rivers, when attached to the stage. The *ceraunoscopium* was a kind of moveable tower, whence Jupiter darted lightning, supposed to be the Greek fire, as in Ajax Oielus. The machine for thunder (*bronton*) was a brazen vase, concealed under the stage, in which they rolled stones. Festus calls it the

Claudian thunder, from Claudius Pulcher, the inventor. The most dreadful machines were, however, the *pegmata* (a general term also for all the machines), which first consisted of scaffolds in stories, &c. These first exhibited criminals fighting at the top, and then, dropping to pieces, precipitated them to the lower story, to be torn to pieces by wild beasts. Sometimes they were for vomiting flames, &c. The *theologium* was a place more elevated than the stage, where the gods stood and spoke, and the machines which held them rested.

The seats of the spectators were divided into stories, each containing seven rows of seats, with two passages (*praecinctiones*) around them above and below. Small staircases divided the seats into sections, called *cunei*, and ended in a gate at the top, which communicated with passages (the *vomitoriae*) for admission.

CHAPTER VI. ROMAN THEATRES

—DESCRIPTION—"DEADHEADS"—PANTOMIME IN ITALY—
LIVIUS ANDRONICUS—*FABULAE ATELLANAE*—
EXTEMPORAL COMEDY—ORIGIN OF THE MASQUE, OPERA,
AND VAUDEVILLE—ORIGIN OF THE TERM HISTRIONIC—
ETRUSCANS—POPULARITY OF PANTOMIME IN ITALY—
PANTOMIMISTS BANISHED BY TRAJAN—NERO AS A
MIME—PYLADES AND BATHYLLUS—SUBJECTS CHOSEN
FOR THE ROMAN PANTOMIMES—THE BALLET—THE *MIMI*
AND *PANTOMIMI*—*ARCHIMIMUS*—VESPASIAN—
HARLEQUIN—"MR. PUNCH"—ZANY, HOW THE WORD
ORIGINATED—ANCIENT MASKS—LUCIAN, CASSIODORUS,
AND DEMETRIUS IN PRAISE OF PANTOMIME—A
CELEBRATED *MIMA*—PANTOMIMES DENOUNCED BY
EARLY WRITERS—THE PURITY OF THE ENGLISH STAGE
CONTRASTED WITH THAT OF THE GRECIAN AND ROMAN—
FEMALE PARTS ON THE GRECIAN AND ROMAN STAGES—
THE PRINCIPAL ROMAN *MIMAS*—THE ORIGIN OF THE
CLOWN OF THE EARLY ENGLISH DRAMA.

The Roman theatres (continues Fosbroke) were of a similar D form. Two lofty arched doorways entered into the pit. In front of the stage, which was very shallow, was a pew-like orchestra. The proscenium was very narrow, and instead of a drop scene was the *elisium*, a house, narrow, with a kind of bow window front in the centre, and a door on each side: for Pollux says that a house with two stories formed part of the stage, whence old women and panders used to look down and peep about them. Within the house were apartments. Around the back of the stage was a *porticus*. At Herculaneum, on a balustrade which divided the orchestra from the stage, was found a row of statues, and on each side of the *pulpitum*, an equestrian figure. Below the theatre (great and small) was a large square constructed, says Vitruvius, for the reception of the audience in bad weather. It consisted of Doric columns, around an open area, forming an ample portico for this purpose, whilst under it were arranged *cellae*, or apartments, amongst which were a soap manufactory, oil mill, corn mill, and prison. An inner *logia* was connected with a suite of apartments. There was also an *exedra*, or recess.

Among the Romans, theatrical approbation was signified by an artificial musical kind of noise, made by the audience to express satisfaction. There were three species of applause denominated from the different noises made in them, viz.: *Bombus*, *Imbrius*, and *Testae*.

First, a confused din, made either by the hands or mouth. The second and third, by beating on a sort of sounding vessel placed in the theatres for that purpose. Persons were instructed to give applause with skill—and there were even masters who professed to teach the art. The proficients in this way let themselves out for hire to the poets, actors, &c., and were so disposed as to support a loud applause. These they called *Laudicena*. At the end of the play, a loud peal of applause was expected, and even asked of the audience either by the chorus or by the person who spoke last. The formula was "*Spectatore Claudite*," or "*Valete et Plaudite*."

The applauders were divided into *Chori*, and disposed in theatres opposite to each other, like the choristers in cathedrals, so that there was a kind of concert of applause. The free admission tickets were small ivory death's heads, and specimens of these are to be seen in the Museum of Naples. From this custom, it is stated, that we derive our word "Deadhead," as denoting one who has a free entrance to places of amusement.

With the dawn of the Roman Empire, Pantomime, in Italy, is first authentically mentioned. The Emperor Augustus always displayed great favour to the Art, and even by some writers he has been credited with being the originator of Pantomime. This, of course, as we have seen, is impossible, and to use a familiar and trite saying, the Pantomimic Art is "as old as the hills" themselves. Again, Bathyllus and Pylades (both freed slaves, the former born in Cilicia, and the latter came from Alexandria), and Hylas, the principal exponents of Pantomime during the reign of Augustus, have also been credited with the honour of originating Pantomime.

The early Roman entertainments only consisted of the military and sacred dances, and the scenes in the circus. With the advent of the arts of Greece the austerity hitherto practised by the Romans, which had arisen, says Duray, "Much more from poverty than conviction," for "Two or three generations had sufficed to change a city which had only known meagre festivities and rustic delights into the home of revelry and pleasure."

With the Romans, in their Pantomimic entertainments, the whole gamut of the emotions were gone through.

When the Greek drama was brought into Rome by Livius Andronicus, the *Fabulae Atellanae*, or *Laudi Osci*—derived from the town of Atella, in Campania, between Capua and Naples—was still employed to furnish the Interludes, and just in a similar way as the *Satyra* Extemporal Interludes supplied the Grecian stage. None of these Atellan Farces have been committed to us, but Cicero, in a letter to his friend Papyrius Paetus, speaks of them as the "More delicate burlesque of the old Atellan Farces." From them also, we derive the Extemporal Comedy, or *Comedia del' Arte* of Italy (afterwards to be noted), with its characters, Harlequin, Clown, Pierrot, and the like, associated with English and Italian Pantomime, and the progenitor also of all those light forms of entertainment known as the Masque, the Opera, and the Vaudeville. On English dramatic literature the Italian Extemporal Comedies and their Pantomimical characters have also had a considerable amount of influence.

Livy mentions that actors were sent for (*circa* 364 B.C.) from Etruria, who, without verses or any action expressive of verses, danced not ungracefully, after the Tuscan manner to the flute. In process of time the Roman youth began to imitate these dancers intermixing raillery with unpolished verses, their gestures corresponding with the sense of the words. Thus were these plays received at Rome, and being improved and refined by frequent performance the Roman actors acquired the name of *Histriones*, from the Etruscan *Hister*, meaning a dancer or a stage player. (From this we obtain our words histrion and histrionic). But their dialogue did not consist of unpremeditated and coarse jests in such rude verses as were used by the *Fescennini*, but of satires, accompanied with music set to the flute, recited with suitable gestures. After satires, which had afforded the people subject of coarse mirth and laughter, were, by this regulation, reduced to form and acting, by degrees became an art, the Roman youth left it to players by profession, and began, as formerly, to act farces at the end of their regular pieces. These dramas were called *Exodia*, and were generally woven with the *Atellanae* Comedies. These were borrowed from the Osci, and were always acted by the Roman youth. Tacitus speaks of *Atellanae* Comedies written in the spirit and language of the Osci having been acted in his time.

It is thought that the Etruscans possessed histories, poems, and dramas, and, if these, then certainly they knew the Pantomimic Art, out of which, in all probability, their dramatic entertainments grew. To the Etruscans the Romans owe their early civilization.

The Etruscan era is supposed to have commenced about 1044 B.C., and we are told that the Etruscans shared with the Greeks, and the Phoenicians, the maritime supremacy of the Mediterranean. In the sepulchral chambers of the Necropolis of Tarquinii, which extends for many miles, there are several scenes painted in the archaic style by the Etruscans, representing the Chase, the Circus, and Dancing Girls.

Soon after its innovation among the Romans, Pantomime spread all over Italy and the provinces. So attractive did it become in Rome, and so popular, that Tiberius issued a decree forbidding the knights and nobles to frequent their houses of entertainment, or to be seen walking in the streets with them. Trajan also oppressed and banished the Pantomimists. Under Caligula, however, they were received with great favour, and Aurelius made them priests of Apollo. Nero, who carried everything to the extremity of foolishness, was not content in patronising the Pantomimes, but must needs assist, and appear himself, as a *Mimi*. Here again, in Nero, another claimant as the author of Pantomime has been put forward.

"So great (observes Gaston Vuillier, in his 'History of Dancing,') was the admiration for Pylades and Bathyllus that the theatrical supporters clothed themselves in different liveries, and broils in the public streets were of frequent occurrence." "The rivalries of Pylades and Bathyllus," says De Laulnaye, "occupied the Romans as much as the gravest affairs of state. Every citizen was a Bathyllian or a Pyladian." Augustus reproved Pylades on one occasion for his quarrels with Bathyllus. The Mime retorted, "It is well for you that the people are engrossed by our disputes; their attention is thus diverted from your actions." A bold retort, but it shows how important these Mimes were. The banishment of Pylades brought about an insurrection, and the Emperor had to recall him.

Cassius attributes the disgrace of Pylades to the intrigues of Bathyllus, Suetonius to his effrontery; for on one occasion, when acting Hercules, annoyed by the criticism of the spectators, he tore off his mask, and shouted to them: "Fools, I am acting a madman." They thought his gestures too extravagant. Another time he shot off arrows amongst the spectators. Amongst other privileges extended by the Emperor Augustus to the *Mimis* was being exempt from magisterial control and immunity from military serving.

The subjects chosen for the Roman Pantomimes, like those of the Grecian mysteries, from which they doubtless were borrowed, were of a Mythological description, and they were of such a nature that the audience could follow them easily, even if they were not already previously acquainted with them. Between the Roman Pantomime, and the Western *ballet d'action*, there is hardly any difference. The Romans always liked to see their stages well peopled; and to help in the action of their Pantomimes, a chorus accompanied with music, formed part of the entertainment. The *Mimis and Mimas*, like the ballet of the present day, provided the dances in addition to their Pantomimic Art of posing and posturing.

Mr. Isaac Disraeli, in his work, "Curiosities of Literature," edited by the late Earl of Beaconsfield, thus distinguishes between the *Mimi* and the *Pantomimi* of the Ancients. The *Mimi* were an impudent race of buffoons who excelled in mimicry, and like our domestic fools, were admitted into convivial parties to entertain the guests. Their powers enabled them to perform a more extraordinary office; for they appear to have been introduced into funerals to mimic the person, and even the language of the deceased. Suetonius describes an *archimimus* accompanying the funeral of Vespasian. This *archimimus* performed his part admirably, not only representing the person, but imitating, according to custom, *ut est mos*, the manners and language of the living Emperor. He contrived a happy stroke at the prevailing foible of Vespasian, when he enquired the cost of all this funeral pomp—"Ten million of sesterces!" On this he observed that if they would give him but a hundred thousand they might throw his body into the Tiber.

The *Pantomimi* were quite of a different class. They were tragic actors, and usually mute; they combined the arts of gesture, music, and dances of the most impressive character. Their silent language has often drawn tears by the pathetic emotions they excited; "Their very nod speaks, their hands talk, and their fingers have a voice," says one of their admirers.

These Pantomimists seem to have been held in great honour. The tragic and the comic masks were among the ornaments of the sepulchral monuments of an *Archmime* and a *Pantomimi*. Montfaucon conjectures that they formed a select fraternity.

The parti-coloured hero (Harlequin), with every part of his dress, has been drawn out of the greatest wardrobe of antiquity; he was a Roman Mime. Harlequin is described with his shaven head (*rasis capitibus*); his sooty face (*fuligine faciem abducti*); his flat unshod feet, (*planipedes*), and his patched coat of many colours, (*Mimi centunculo*). Even *Pulcinello*, whom we familiarly call "Punch," may receive, like other personages of no great importance, all his dignity from antiquity; one of his Roman ancestors having appeared to an antiquary's visionary eye in a bronze statue; more than one erudite dissertation authenticates the family likeness; the nose long, prominent and hooked; the staring goggle eyes; the hump at his back, and at his breast; in a word, all the character which so strongly marks the Punch race, as distinctly as whole dynasties have been featured by the Austrian lip and the Bourbon nose.

The genealogy of the whole family is confirmed by the general term which includes them all: in English, Zany; in Italian, *Zanni*; in the Latin, *Sannio*; and a passage in "Cicero *De Oratore*," paints Harlequin and his brother gesticulators after the life; the perpetual trembling motion of their limbs, their ludicrous and flexible gestures, and all the mimicry of their faces: "*Quid enim potest tam ridiculum quam Sannio esse? Qui ore vultu, imitandis motibus, voce, denique corpore ridetur ipso.*" Lib II., Sect. 51. ("For what has more of the ludicrous than Sannio? Who, with his mouth, his face, imitating every motion with his voice, and, indeed, with all his body, provokes laughter.")

The Latin Sannio was changed by the Italians into (as Ainsworth explains) Zanni, as, in words like Smyrna and Sambuco, they change the s into z, which gives Zmyrna and Zambuco, and hence we derive our word Zany. The word is, however, originally obtained from the Greek *Sannos* (observes Quadrio), from whence the Latins derived their *Sannio*.

From the size of the ancient theatres it was not possible to notice the visage of the actors, and this was one, but not the only reason, why masks were adopted. The Ancients did not like a character to be attempted, to which a proper appropriation was not annexed, and these masks were so contrived, that the profile on one side exhibited chagrin, and on the other serenity, or whatever other passion was most required. The actor thus, according to the part he was playing, presented the side of the mask best suited to the passage which he was reciting. The large mouths of these masks were presumed to have contained some bronze instrument suited to assist the voice, upon the principle of the speaking trumpet; for the mask was wider, and the recitation in tragedy much louder than in comedy, so that the voice might be heard all over the theatre. The masks of the dancers were of regular features.

By some it has been contended that these masks covered both the head and the shoulders under the supposed idea that when the head was thus enlarged it would throw the whole body into symmetry when raised upon stilts. It has, also, been argued that the masks for some of the characters were made of gold-beaters skin, or some transparent substance just covering the face so that the facial muscles could be seen through it, and the eyes, mouth, and ears being left uncovered. These masks, however, delineated very carefully the features of the character that were to be represented. Something not unlike the huge Pantomime masks of a hideous and frightful shape that we sometimes see in our present day Pantomimes must have appeared, especially those that covered the head and shoulders of the *Mimis* in the days of the Romans. Those that were just of the size of the face in all probability were fantastic and picturesque; and the third and remaining species of mask made of a transparent substance could hardly have been very effective.

Mr. Wright tells us, in his book on the Chester Mystery plays (which work I shall again refer to later on), that masks were used in the Mystery series of plays acted in England during the thirteenth and fourteenth centuries.

Julius Pollux is still more ample in his account of theatrical masks used in Tragedy, Satyr, and Comedy. Niobe weeping, Medea furious, Ajax astonished, and Hercules enraged. In Comedy, the slave, the parasite, the clown, the captain, the old woman, the harlot, the austere old man, the debauched young man, the prodigal, the prudent young woman, the matron, and the father of a family, were all constantly characterised by particular masks.

Lucian and the other writers of the Augustan era, have handed down to us sufficient information to show how Pantomime in Rome was so highly thought of. Cassiodorous, speaking of them, says:—"Men whose eloquent hands had a tongue, as it were, on the tip of each finger—men who spoke while they were silent, and knew how to make a recital without opening their mouths—men, in short, whom Polyhymnia had formed in order to show that there was no necessity for articulation in order to convey our thoughts." Demetrius, a cynic philosopher, laughed at the Romans for permitting so strange an entertainment; but having been, with much difficulty, prevailed upon to be present at the representation of one of them, he was confounded with wonder. The story represented was that of Mars and Venus, the whole performed by a single actor, who described the fable in *dumb show*. At length the philosopher, wrought up to the highest pitch of admiration, exclaimed, "That the actor *had no occasion for a tongue, he spoke so well with his hands*."

Of one Pontus, who had come on a visit to Nero, we are told that he was present at a performance, in the course of which a favourite Mime gave a representation of the Labours of Hercules. The Mime's gestures were so precise that he could follow the action without the slightest hesitation. Being struck by the performance, on taking leave he begged Nero to give him the actor, explaining that there was a barbarous tribe adjoining his dominions, whose language no one could learn, and that Pantomime could express his intentions to them so faithfully by gestures that they would at once understand.

The dress of the performers of Pantomime was made to reveal, and not to conceal, their figures. After the second century women began to act in their representations, and even down to the sixth century we find them associating themselves with Pantomime, and mention is made of a celebrated *Mima*, who was ultimately raised to the imperial throne. Through the lewdness of the *Mimis* and *mimas* in Pantomime, their dress, or rather lack of dress, Pantomimes were denounced, not only by the early Christian writers, but also by some of the Pagan writers, like Juvenal, as being very prejudicial to morality.

It has, however, always been a favourite topic of the Prynne's, the Jeremy Collier's and the Dr. Style's, and such like opponents of the theatre, to contrast the English stage with the purity of the Grecian and Roman Theatres. Now, without stopping to enquire whether this has any particular connection with the subject of their dissertations, or whether it is not in fact quite irrelevant to the question, it is impossible not to remark the crass ignorance which these assertions display of the manners and customs of the theatres of either the Greeks or the Romans. Without wearying the reader by entering into a long discussion upon the subject, it will be sufficient to recall certain passages in Aristophanes, Xenophon, Plautus, and Terence to induce them to hesitate in assenting to such vague assertions of the purity of either the Grecian or Roman dramatic writers. William Prynne, the English Puritan writer, in his violent attack on the stage in the "Histrio-Mastix" or "Players Scourge"—which book, by the way, for some unfavourable comments therein on the Queen of Charles I., and the ladies of her Court, for attending theatrical representations, was debarred his rooms (he was a barrister), by the Court of Star Chamber, sentenced to be imprisoned for life, fined £5,000, committed to the Tower, placed in the pillory, both ears cut off, and his book burnt by the common hangman; yet after undergoing all these pains and penalties, he published a recantation of all that he had previously written in his "Histrio-Mastix"—says "It seems that the Grecian actors did now and then to refresh the spectators, bring a kind of cisterne on the stage, wherein naked women did swim and bathe themselves between the acts and scenes; which wicked, impudent, and execrable practice the holy father Chrysostom doth sharpely and excellently declaime against."

Xenophon mentions the tale of "Bacchus and Ariadne," Pantomimically played, and Martial tells us he saw the whole story of "Pasiphae," minutely represented on the stage of the Mimis, and Plautus, in his epilogue to "Casina," has—

"Nunc vos aequim est, manibus meritis,

Meritam mercedem dare.

Qui faxit, clam uxorem, ducat scortum

Semper quod volet.

Verum qui non manibus clare, quantum

Potent, plauserit,

Ei, pro scorto, supponetur hircus unctus nantea."

On the Roman stage female parts were represented in tragedy by men, is ascertained (says Malone) by one of Cicero's letters to Atticus, and by a passage in Horace. Horace mentions, however, a female performer called Arbuscula, but as we find from his own authority men personated women on the Roman stage, she was probably an *Emboliariae*. Servius calls her a *Mima*, or one who danced in the Pantomimic dances, and which seems more probable, as she is mentioned by Cicero, who says the part of Andromache was played by a male performer on the very day Arbuscula also performed.

The principal Roman *Mimas* were:—Arbuscula, Thymele, Licilia, Dionysia, Cytheris, Valeria, and Cloppia.

In the satirical interludes of the Grecian stage, and the *Fabulae Atellanae* of the Roman theatres, the *Exodiarii* and *Emboliariae* of the Mimes, were the remote progenitors (says Malone) of the Vice or Devil, and the Clown of our English Mystery plays, the latter series of plays being the origin of the drama of this country. The exact conformity between our Clown and the *Exodiarii* and *Emboliariae* of the Roman stage is ascertained by that passage in Pliny— "*Lucceia Mima centum annis in scena pronuntiavit. Galeria,*

Copiola, Emboliariae, reducta est in scenam: annum certissimum quartum agens," is thus translated by an English author, Philemon Holland, "Lucceia, a common Vice in a play, followed the stage, and acted thereupon 100 yeeres. Such another Vice that *plaied the foole, and made sporte between whiles in interludes*, named Galeria Copiola, was brought to act upon the stage when she was in the 104th yeere of her age." We shall, in another chapter, return to the Vice, or Clown.

CHAPTER VII. INTRODUCTION OF THE ROMAN PANTOMIMIC ART INTO BRITAIN

—FIRST ENGLISH REFERENCE TO THE WORD PANTOMIME—THE FALL OF THE ROMAN EMPIRE—THE SACRED PLAY—CORNISH AMPHITHEATRES— PANTOMIMICAL AND LYRICAL ELEMENTS IN THE SACRIFICE OF THE MASS—CHRISTIAN BANISHMENT OF THE *MIMIS*—PENALTIES IMPOSED BY THE CHURCH—ST. ANTHONY ON HARLEQUIN AND PUNCH—VANDENHOFF— WHAT WE OWE TO THE *MIMIS*.

With the advent of Julius Caesar and the conquest of Britain by the Romans, about the year 52 B.C., we have, in all probability, the first introduction of the Roman Pantomimic Art into this country. Inasmuch as we have it upon the authority of history that Caesar travelled with his Mimes, and it is, therefore, not improbable that they came into Britain with him. England, then, during the occupancy of the Romans, must have known the Dramatic Art, or else (as Dibdin observes) Pacuvius, Accius, and Livius Andronicus were ignorant of it. Martial tells us that it did, and so does Boadicea, so that we have not only Roman authorities for it, but also British.

The word "Pantomime" could not, I may say here, have been Anglicised earlier than sometime during the seventeenth century. Dr. Johnson's earliest example is from "Hudibras"—

"Not that I think those *Pantomimes*,

Who vary action with the times,

Are less ingenious in their art

Than those who duly act one part."

Bacon and Ben Jonson use the Latin *Pantomimi*—"Here be certain *Pantomimi* that will represent the voices of players." Again in the "Masque of Love's Triumph," etc., 1630, "After the manner of the old *Pantomimi* they dance over a distracted Comedy of Love."

The fall of the Roman Empire and the progress of Christianity in Europe sounded the death knell of Paganism and its attributes, of which Pantomime was deemed to be one, owing to the bad odour in which this form of entertainment had got to during the last days of the Empire. Notwithstanding this the church was only too glad to avail itself of Pantomime as a vehicle to portray before the world at large, and in order to turn attention to the great moral truths to be deduced from the death of Him on Calvary Hill. These exhibitions of religious subjects, in the form of *tableaux vivants*, took place in the churches, and, having regard to the sacred edifices in which they were given, they were, especially in the beginning, I conjecture, performed in dumb show, without any dialogue. Afterwards dialogue was introduced, and they began to be, not only held in the churches, but also in the church-yards, the streets, and in booths.

It is true the sacred play was not a new institution, as one is said to be mentioned about the time of the Fall of Jerusalem. In Cornwall, plays were given in the ancient times in the open air, after the fashion of the Roman Amphitheatre, with the dialogue in the Cymric tongue. Pantomimical performances might also have been given in those open-air theatres by the Romans.

Perhaps no better example of the early Sacred Drama I can give, and which is still with us, and performed daily, is the sacrifice of the Mass in all Roman Catholic Churches throughout the length and breadth of the world. In the Mass we have a dramatic action *pantomimically* presented, in part aided by lyrical and epical elements. I will not, however, pursue this portion of my subject further, save than to add that at the Catholic Churches' festivals, especially during Holy Week or Passion Week, what I have mentioned of the Mass becomes at these times marked in even a greater degree.

With the decline and fall of the Roman Empire, the *Mimis* became wanderers on the face of the earth, only appearing at festivals and the like, when they were wanted, and returning to their haunts as mysteriously as they came.

In the fourth century A.D. they were excluded from the benefit of the rites of the Church, and even those who visited their entertainments, instead of churches, on the Sundays and holidays, were excommunicated. The Theodosian creed provided that the actors were not to have the sacraments administered to them save when death was imminent, and then only that, in case of recovery, their calling should be renounced.

In the second century one of the Fathers of the Church wrote a special treatise against plays (*Tertulian De Spectaculis*), in which he asks those who will not renounce them "Whether the God of truth, who hates all falsehood, can be willing to receive into His kingdom those whose features and hair, whose age and sex, whose sighs and laughter, love and anger, are all feigned. He promises them a tragedy of their own when, in the day of Judgment, they shall be consigned to everlasting suffering."

However, the church was not always against the stage, even in those early times, as St. Thomas Aquinas says that "The office of the player as being serviceable for the enlivenment of men, and as not being blameworthy if the player leads an upright life." Both Saints Thomas Aquinas and Anthony supported the stage, the latter only stipulating that the character of Harlequin should not be represented by a clergyman, nor that Punch should be exhibited in church.

It is one of the most remarkable things that, despite the bitterness, hostility, and deadly enmity that has been levelled at the stage, and its players termed "Rogues and Vagabonds" from time immemorial, how it has lived through it all. In connection with this how the lines of that great actor, Vandenhoff, occurs to me, a few of which, with the reader's permission, I subjoin.

"The drama's now a great established fact,

That can't be blink'd, ignored how'er attack'd

By vain abuse or angry prejudice;

The time's gone by when *playing was a vice*;

When bigots mark'd the actor with a ban,

(Tho' saintly crowds to hear his accents ran),

Denied him sacred rite and hallowed grave—

Filching from God the soul he made to save—

And, for the pleasure which his life had giv'n

On earth, refused him dead, a place in heav'n.

No! wiser days bring gentler feelings in,

And 'Nature's touches makes the whole world kin'."

By degrees the *Mimis*, or mummers, with their fellows, spread themselves all over Europe. The humbler of the craft, in fact it might be said of them all, as Othello's occupation had (for them) long since been gone, strolled from castle to castle, from village to town, and earning their livelihood as best they could. To these wandering Bohemians we owe such traditions of the drama that survived with them into succeeding ages; and to them also we are indebted for keeping alive by inculcating unto others the Art of *Pantomimus*, when in the heyday of its popularity in the Roman Empire.

CHAPTER VIII. PANTOMIME IN THE ENGLISH MYSTERY OR MIRACLE PLAYS AND PAGEANTS—A RETROSPECT OF THE EARLY DRAMA

—MYSTERIES ON BIBLICAL EVENTS—CHESTER, COVENTRY, YORK, AND TOWNELEY MYSTERY PLAYS— PLAYS IN CHURCHES—TRACES OF THE MYSTERY PLAY IN ENGLAND IN THE NINETEENTH CENTURY—MYSTERY PLAYS ON THE CONTINENT—THE CHESTER SERIES OF PLAYS—THE DEVIL OR CLOWN AND THE *EXODIARII* AND *EMBOLIARIAE* OF THE ANCIENT MIMES.

It is presumed that, not only were the early sacred plays acted in dumb-show, but that the Miracle or Mysteries of Religion series of plays—which grew out of the sacred play—also the Pageants in the beginning, and for long afterwards were acted in this wise. Percy, in his "Reliques of Ancient English Poetry," also takes this view. He says:— "They were (the Mysteries) probably a kind of *dumb show*, intermingled, it may be, with a few short speeches, at length they grew into regular scenes of connected dialogues, formally divided into acts and scenes." Colley Cibber has: "It has been conjectured that the actors of the Mysteries of Religion were *mummers*, a word signifying one who makes and disguises himself to play the fool *without speaking*. They were dressed in an antic manner, *dancing, mimicking,* and *showing postures*." Mr. Wright also observes (in his work on the Mystery Plays of Chester, published by the Shakespearean Society) that the "*chief effect seems to have been caused by the dumb show.*"

Before dealing with the Mysteries, and as perhaps a kind of retrospect, let us have a look what Wharton has to say of the early drama. "Trade," he says (in the early centuries) "was carried on by means of fairs, which lasted several days. Charlemagne established many great marts of this sort in France, as did William the Conqueror and his Norman successors in England. The merchants, who frequented these fairs in numerous caravans and companies, employed every art to draw the people together. They were, therefore, accompanied by jugglers, minstrels, and buffoons (*i.e.*, Pantomimists), who were no less interested in giving their attendance and exercising their skill on these occasions. Few large towns existed, no public spectacles or popular amusements were established; and as the sedentary pleasures of domestic life and private society were yet unknown, the fair time was the season for diversion. In proportion as the shows were attended and encouraged, they began to be set off with new decorations and improvements; and the arts of buffoonery being rendered still more attractive by extending their circle of exhibition, acquired an importance in the eyes of the people. By degrees the Clergy, observing that the entertainments of dancing, music, and mimicry exhibited at these annual celebrations made the people less religious by promoting idleness and a love of festivity, proscribed these sports and excommunicated the performers."

Mystery plays were afterwards divided into three classes, though the generic term Mysteries, meaning all three, is generally used. In the Mysteries, Biblical events were principally used; Miracle plays were obtained from the legends of the saints; and the last, Moralities, allegorical stories of a moral character not essentially taken from the Bible, or from the legends of the saints, comprised the third heading. The Mysteries were for several centuries known on the Continent before they were performed in England. The earliest Mystery play known to have been acted in England was at Dunstable about the year 1110. It was probably in Latin, and composed by a Norman monk.

It is a peculiarity of the English Mystery plays that they were combined into a series of plays on the Old and New Testament; and in which the whole course of Divine Providence, from the Creation to the Day of Judgment, is set before the spectator. Four noted groups of plays were the Chester, the Towneley, Coventry, and York Mystery plays. The Chester plays began on Whit Monday, and, continued till the following Wednesday. Permission to perform them, in the beginning of their institution, had twice to be asked of the Pope. They consisted of 24 plays, and were almost annually performed till 1577. Before the suppression of the monasteries the Grey Friars at Coventry were celebrated for their exhibitions of the Mystery plays usually on *Corpus Christi*. The Towneley, or Woodkirk group of plays were acted at Woodkirk, about four miles from Wakefield, and they are of a style that may be likened to the times of Henry VI., or Edward IV. Until the Mystery play fell into disuse, the trading companies and guilds seem principally to have maintained them. The mixture of secular with ecclesiastical players helped to change the characters of the English plays and to provoke censure, which began to be levelled at them from the beginning of the thirteenth century.

The practise of performing plays in sacred edifices in England, had not ceased in 1542, when Bishop Bonner prohibited them in his diocese. However, so late as 1572, it appears that Interludes were occasionally performed in Churches.

Collier speaks of a kind of Mystery, or Miracle play, exhibited in the last century, with the characters of Herod, Beelzebub, and others. In 1838 Sandy mentions of having seen the play of "St. George and the Dragon," presented in the Northern and Western parts of the Kingdom, or rather Queendom, as Victoria had just ascended the throne. I myself remember quite well, within a couple of decades ago, what was probably at the time a remnant of the old Mystery play presented in a rural part of Lancashire by men in a fantastic garb, and termed by the country folk, "Paste-eggers." They generally appeared about Good Friday and on to Easter; and their performance consisted of a mixture of music (?), songs, and sometimes not over choice language. This custom does not now exist where I write of, but it may do—though I very much doubt—in some rural parts. On the Continent, as at Oberammergau, Mystery plays are still enacted.

The following account of the Chester Mysteries may be of interest, and appears (says Warton) in the Harleian Catalogue. M.S. Harl. 2013, etc. Exhibited at Chester in the year 1327 at the expense of the different trading companies of that city. "The Fall of Lucifer," by the tanners; "The Creation," by the drapers; "The Deluge," by the dyers; "Abraham, Melchizedeck and Lot," by the barbers; "Moses, Balak and Balaam," by the cappers; "The Salutation and the Nativity," by the wrights (carpenters); "The Shepherds feeding the Flocks by Night," by the painters and glaziers; "The Three Kings," by the vintners; "The oblation of the Three Kings," by the mercers; "The Killing of the Holy Innocents," by the goldsmiths; "The Purification," by the blacksmiths; "The Temptations," by the butchers; "The Blindmen and Lazarus," by the glovers; "Jesus and the Lepers," by the cowesarys; "Christ's Passion," by the bowyers, fletchers and ironmongers; "Descent into Hell," by the cooks and inn-keepers; "Resurrection," by the skinners; "Ascension," by the taylors; "The Election of St. Matthias," "Sending of the Holy Ghost," etc., by the fishmongers; "Anti-christ," by the clothiers; and "The Day of Judgment," by the websters (weavers). The reader will perhaps smile at some of these combinations. This is the substance and order of the former part of the play. God enters, creating the world, he breathes life into Adam, leads him into Paradise, and opens his side while sleeping. Adam and Eve appear *naked*, and *not ashamed*; and the old Serpent enters, lamenting his fall. He converses with Eve. She eats part of the forbidden fruit, and gives part to Adam. They propose, according to the stage directions, to make themselves, *subligacula a folis quibus tegamus pudenda*, cover their nakedness with leaves and converse with God. God's curse. The Serpent exits, hissing. They are driven from Paradise by four angels, and the Cherubim with a flaming sword. Adam appears digging the ground, and Eve spinning. Their children, Cain and Abel, enter, the former kills his brother. Adam's lamentation. Cain is banished, etc., etc.

Adam and Eve, in the "altogether," so to speak, were acted like this as late as the sixteenth century. In a play called "The Travails of the Three English Brothers," acted in 1607, there occurs this:—

"Many idle toyes, but the old play *that Adam and Eve acted in bare action under the figge tree draws most of the gentlemen.*"

An Account of the Proclamation of the Mystery plays, acted in "Ye Citye on ye Dee," may prove of interest, and the copy of which I subjoin is taken from the Harleian M.S. No. 2013.

"The proclamation for Whitsone playes made by Wm. Newell, Clarke of the Pendice, 24 Hen. 8. Wm. Snead 2nd yere Maior."

"For as much as auld tyme, not only for the augmentation and increese of the holy and catholick faith of our Saviour Jesu Christ, and to exort the mindes of comon people to good devotion and holsome doctrine thereof, but also for the comonwelth and prosperity of this citty, a play and declaration of divers storyes of Bible beginning with the Creation and fall of Lucifer, and ending with the generall Judgment of the world, to be declared and played in Whitsonne weeke, was devised and made by one Sir Henry

Frances, sometyme moonck of this monastrey disolved, who obtayning and gat of Clemant, then Bushop of Rome, a 1000 dayes of pardon, and of the Bushop of Chester at that tyme 40 dayes of pardon, graunted from thensforth to every person resorting, in peaceable manner with good devotion, to heare and see the sayd playes, from time to time as oft as they shall be played within the said citty (and that every person or persons disturbing the sayd playes in the maner wise to be acused by the authority of the sayd pope Clemant's bulls, untill such tyme as he or they be absolved thereof) which playes were devised to the honor of God by John Arnway, then maior of this citty of Chester, his brethren and whole cominalty thereof, to be brought forth, declared, and played, at the cost and charges of the craftesman and occupations of the sayd citty, which hitherto have from tyme to tyme used and performed the same accordingly.

"Wherefore Mr. maior, in the King's name, stratly chargeth and commandeth that every person and persons of what estate, degree, or condition so ever he or they be resorting to the sayd playes, do use themselves peaciblie, without making any assault, affray, or other disturbance, whereby the same playes shall be disturbed, and that no manner of person or persons, whiche so ever he or they be, do use or wear any unlawfull weapons within the precinct of the sayd citty during the tyme of the sayd playes (not only upon payn of cursing by authority of the sayd Pope Clemant's bulls but also) upon payn of imprisonment of their bodyes, and making fine to the King at Mr. maior's pleasure."

Archdeacon Rogers, who died in 1595, and saw the Whitsuntide plays performed at Chester in the preceding year, gives the following account of the mode of exhibition:—

"The time of the yeare they were played was on Monday, Tuesday, and Wenseday in Whitson weake. The maner of these playes weare every company had his pagiant, or parte, which pagiants weare a high scafolde with 2 rowmes, a higher and a lower, upon 4 wheeles. In the lower they apparelled themselves, and in the higher rowme they played, being all open on the tope, that all behoulders might heare and see them. The places where they played them was in every streete. They begane first at the abay gates, and when the first pagiante was played, it was wheeled to the high crosse before the mayor, and soe to every streete; and soe every streete had a pagiant playinge before them at one time, till all the pagiantes for the daye appoynted weare played, and when one pagiant was neere ended, word was broughte from streete to streete that soe they mighte come in place thereof exceedinge orderlye, and all the streetes have their pagiantes afore them all at one time playeinge togeather; to se which playes was greate resorte, and also scafoldes and stages made in the streetes in those places where they determined to playe their pagiantes."

Strutt has the following description of the Mystery plays:— "In the early dawn of literature, and when the sacred Mysteries were the only theatrical performances, what is now called the stage did then consist of three several platforms or stages, raised one above another; on the uppermost sat the *Pater Caelestis*, surrounded with his angels; on the second appeared the holy saints and glorified men; and the last and lowest were occupied by mere men who had not passed through this life to the regions of eternity. On one side of this lowest platform was the resemblance of a dark pitchy cavern, from whence issued appearance of fire and flames; and when it was necessary the audience were treated with hideous yellings and noises, as imitations of the howlings and cries of the wretched souls tormented by the relentless demons. From this yawning cave the devils themselves constantly ascended, to delight and instruct the spectators; to delight because they were usually the greatest jesters and buffoons that then appeared; and to instruct for that they treated the wretched mortals who were delivered to them with the utmost cruelty, warning thereby all men carefully to avoid the falling into the clutches of such hardened and relentless spirits."

It is interesting to note that Hell was imitated by a whale's open jaws, behind which a fire was lighted, in such a way, however, so as not to injure the "damned," who had to pass into its gaping mouth. The performer who impersonated God had not only his face but also the hair of his wig gilded. Christ was dressed in a long sheep's skin. The Devil, or Vice (the *Exodiarii* and *Emboliariae* of the ancient *Mimis*), was easily recognisable by his horns and his tail, whilst his beard was of a bright red colour, to indicate the flames of the region in which he dwelt. Judas also wore a wig of a fiery hue, and, after being hung, had sometimes to do the "cock crowing," as some old accounts of the York Mysteries show.

It appears to have been customary for the Devil to appear before the audience with a cry of "Ho! ho! ho!" somewhat similar to the ejaculations of the Pantomime Clown in after years. (See *Gammer Gurton's Needle*, Act II., Sc. 3, and "The Devil is an Ass," by Ben Jonson, Act I., Sc. 1.) The following passage occurs in "Wily Beguiled," 1606. "Tush! feare not the dodge; I'll rather put on my flashing red nose, and my flaming face, and come wrapped in a calfe's skin, and cry 'Ho! ho! ho!'" Again, "I'll put me on my great carnation nose, and wrap me in a rousing calf's-skin suit, and come like some hob-goblin, or some Devil ascended from the grisly pit of hell, and like a scarebabe make him take to his legs; I'll play the Devil, I warrant ye."

CHAPTER IX. THE CLOWN OR FOOL OF THE EARLY ENGLISH DRAMA

—MORALITIES—THE INTERLUDE—THE RISE OF ENGLISH TRAGEDY AND COMEDY—"DUMB SHEWS" IN THE OLD PLAYS—PLAYS SUPPRESSED BY ELIZABETH—A RETROSPECT.

In the sixth chapter of this work, in quoting Malone, I have mentioned that the *Exodiarii* and *Emboliariae* of the *Mimis* were the remote progenitors of the Clown of the Mystery Plays of this country. Now let us see what were the duties the Clown fulfilled in the old plays of this country, and also briefly of the others who were known under the generic name of Clown or fool.

In the early drama the Clown was a personage of no mean importance and whose duty was to preserve the stage from vacancy by amusing the audience with extemporary buffoonery, and also at the end of the performance. And, as Heywood, in his "History of Women" (1624), says "By his mimic gestures to breed in the less capable mirth and laughter." On these occasions, it was usual to descant, in a humourous style, on various subjects proposed to him by the spectators; but they were more commonly entertained with what was termed a jig: this was a ludicrous composition in rhyme, sung by the Clown, accompanied by his pipe and tabor. In these jigs there were sometimes more actors than one, and the most unbounded license of tongue was allowed; the pith of the matter being usually some scurrilous exposure of persons among, or well known to the audience. Here again history repeats itself in this once more, and in imitation of the satirical interludes of the Grecian stage and the *Atellans* and *Mimis* of the Roman theatres.

The practice of putting the fools and Clowns in requisition between the acts and scenes (observes Francis Douce), and after the play was finished, to amuse the spectators with their tricks, may be traced to the Greek and Roman theatres; and their usages being preserved in the middle ages, wherever the Roman influence had spread, it would not, of course, be peculiar to England. The records of the French theatre demonstrate this fact; in the "Mystery of Saint Barbara," we find this stage direction:—*Pausa. Vadunt, et stultus loquitur.* (A pause. They quit the stage, and the fool speaks). And in this way he is frequently brought on between the scenes.

It is quite obvious that the terms Clown and fool were used, though improperly, perhaps, as synonymous by our old dramatists. Their confused introduction might render this doubtful to one who had not well considered the matter. The fool of our early plays denoted a mere idiot or natural, or else a witty hireling retained to make sport for his masters. The Clown was a character of more variety; sometimes he was a mere rustic; and, often, no more than a shrewd domestic. There are instances in which any low character in a play served to amuse with his coarse sallies, and thus became the Clown of the piece. In fact, the fool of the drama was a kind of heterogeneous being, copied in part from real life, but highly coloured in order to produce effect. This opinion derives force from what is put into the mouth of Hamlet, when he admonishes those who perform the Clowns, to speak no more than is set down for them. Indeed, Shakespeare himself cannot be absolved from the imputation of making mere caricatures of his merry Andrews, unless we suppose, what is very probable, that his compositions have been much interpolated with the extemporaneous jokes of the players. To this folly, allusions are made in a clever satire, entitled, "Pasquils Mad-cappe, throwne at the Corruptions of these Times," 1626, quarto.

"Tell country players, that old paltry jests

Pronounced in a painted motley coate,

Filles all the world so full of cuckoo nests,

That nightingales can scarcely sing a note.

Oh! bid them turn their minds to better meanings;

Fields are ill sowne that give no better gleanings."

Sir Philip Sidney reprobates the custom of introducing fools on the stage; and declares that the plays of his time were neither right tragedies nor right comedies, for the authors mingled kings and Clowns, "not," says he, "because the matter so carrieth it, but thrust in the Clowne by head and shoulders to play a part in majestical matters, with neither decencie nor discretion; so as neither the admiration and commisseration, nor the right sportfulnesse, is by their mongrell tragie-comedie obtained." Rankin, a puritan, contemporary with Shakespeare, wrote a most bitter attack on plays and players, whom he calls monsters; "And whie monsters?" says he, "because under colour of humanitie they present nothing but prodigious vanitie; these are wels without water, dead branches fit for fuell, cockle amongst corne, unwholesome weedes amongst sweete hearbes; and, finallie, feends that are crept into the worlde by stealth, and hold possession by subtill invasion." In another place, he says, "some transformed themselves to rogues, others to ruffians, some others to Clownes, a fourth to fools; the rogues were ready, the ruffians were rude, theyr Clownes cladde as well with country condition, as in ruffe russet; theyr fooles as fond as might be."

To give a clear view of our subject, something of the different sorts of fools may be thus classed:

1.—The *general domestic fool*, termed often, but *improperly*, a *Clown*; described by Puttenham as "a buffoune, or counterfett foole."

2.—The *Clown*, who was a mere country booby, or a witty rustic.

3.—The *female fool*, who was generally an idiot.

4.—The *city or corporation fool*, an assistant in public entertainments.

5.—The *tavern fool*, retained to amuse the customers.

6.—The *fool of the ancient Mysteries and Moralities*, otherwise the *Vice*.

7.—The *fool in the old dumb shows*, often alluded to by Shakespeare.

8.—The *fool in the Whitsun ales and morris dance.*

9.—The *mountebank's fool, or merry Andrew.*

There may be others in our ancient dramas, of an irregular kind, not reducible to any of these classes; but to exemplify them is not within the scope of this essay: what has been stated may assist the readers of old plays to judge for themselves when they meet with such characters.

The practice of retaining fools can be distinctly traced from the remotest times. They were to be found alike in the palace and the brothel; the Pope had his fool, and the bawd hers; they excited the mirth of kings and beggars; the hovel of the villain and the castle of the baron were alike exhilarated by their jokes. With respect to the antiquity of this custom in England, it appears to have existed even during the period of our Saxon history, but we are certain of the fact in the reign of William the Conqueror. Maitre Wace, an historian of that time, has an account of the preservation of William's life, when Duke of Normandy, by his fool, *Goles*; and, in Domesday book, mention is made of *Berdin joculator regis*; and though this term sometimes denoted a minstrel, evidence might be adduced to prove, that in this instance it signified a buffoon.

The entertainment, fools were expected to afford, may be collected in great variety from our old plays, especially from those of Shakespeare; but, perhaps, a good idea may be formed of their general conduct from a passage in a curious tract by Lodge, entitled, "Wit's Miserie," 1599, quarto: "Immoderate and disordinate joy became incorporate in the bodie of a jeaster; this fellow in person is comely, in apparell courtly, but in behaviour a very ape, and no man; his studie is to coin bitter jeasts, or to shew antique motions, or to sing baudie sonnets and ballads; give him a little wine in his head, he is continually flearing and making of mouthes; he laughs intemperately at every little occasion, and dances about the house, leaps over tables, outskips men's heads, trips up his companions' heeles, burns sack with a candle, and hath all the feats of a lord of misrule in the countrie: feed him in his humour, you shall have his heart; in mere kindness he will hug you in his armes, kisse you on the cheeke, and rapping out an horrible oath, crie 'God's soule, Tum, I love you, you knowe my poore heart, come to my chamber for a pipe of tobacco, there lives not a man in this world that I more honor.' In these ceremonies you shall know his courting, and it is a speciall mark of him at table, he sits and makes faces: keep not this fellow company, for in jingling with him, your wardropes shall be wasted, your credits crackt, your crownes consumed, and time (the most precious riches of the world) utterly lost."

With regard to the fool's business on the stage, it was nearly the same as in reality, with this difference, that the wit was more highly seasoned. In Middleton's "Mayor of Quinborough," a company of actors, with a Clown, make their appearance, and the following dialogue ensues:—

1st Cheater. This is our Clown, sir.

Simon.   Fye, fye, your company

         Must fall upon him and beat him; he's too fair i'faith,

         To make the people laugh.

1st Cheater. Not as he may be dress'd, sir.

Simon.   Faith, dress him how you will. I'll give him

         That gift, he will never look half scurvily enough.

         Oh! the Clowns that I have seen in my time,

The very peeping out of one of them would have

Made a young heir laugh, though his father lay a-
dying;

A man undone in law the day before,

(The saddest case that can be) might for his second

Have burst himself with laughing, and ended all

His miseries. Here was a merry world, my masters!

Some talk of things of state, of puling stuff;

There's nothing in a play like to a Clown,

If he have the grace to hit on it, that's the thing
indeed.

Away then, shift; Clown, to thy motley crupper.

In the *praeludium* to Goffe's "Careless Shepherdess," 1656, quarto, there is a panegyric on them, and some concern is shown for the fool's absence in the play itself, while it is stated that "The motley coat was banished with trunk-hose." Yet in Charles II.'s reign, some efforts were made to restore the character. In the tragedy of "Thorney Abbey, or the London Maid," 1662, 12mo., the prologue is delivered by a fool, who uses these words:—"The poet's a fool who made the tragedy, to tell a story of a king and a court, and leave a fool out on't, when in Pacey's, and Sommer's, and Patche's, and Archer's times, my venerable predecessours, a fool was alwaies the principal verb." Shadwell's play of "The Woman Captain," 1680, is perhaps the last in which a regular fool is introduced; and even there, his master is made to say that the character was exploded on the stage. In real life, as was formerly stated, the professed fool was to be met with at a much later period, but the custom has long been obsolete.

What I have said of the Mysteries of Religion plays will, I hope, be sufficient to show the reader how they were associated with Pantomime. The Moralities, founded on the Mysteries, were the means used to inculcate, by the aid of a slight plot, religious truths without directly using scriptural or legendary subjects. Malone says of them:—"I am unable to ascertain when the first Morality appeared, but incline to think not sooner than the reign of Edward IV. (about 1460). The public pageants of the reign of his predecessor were uncommonly splendid, and being then *first* enlivened by the introduction of *speaking* allegorical personages, properly and characteristically habited, naturally led the way to these personifications, by which Moralities were *distinguished from* the simple religious dramas called Mysteries."

The Interlude, that was the progenitor of English Comedy, next arrived. The origin of the Interlude is credited to John Heywood.

It is interesting to note that a play, entitled, "Gammer Gurton's Needle," is credited with being our first English Comedy, though its humour and wit, it is stated, is of a low and sordid kind. Others make claim for the comedy, "Ralph Roister Doister."

Tragedy and Comedy now began to raise their heads, yet they could not, for some time, do more than bluster and quibble. There is an excellent criticism on them by that distinguished statesman, poet, scholar, and brave soldier, Sir Philip Sydney. "Some of their pieces were only '*dumb shews*,' some with choruses, and some they explained by an Interlocutor," says an old writer on the subject. The mention of Pantomime in connection with tragedy, and as an example how Pantomime was requisitioned in Shakespeare's time, is shown in the Second Scene of Act

III. of "Hamlet," wherein the "dumb shew" is given by the players.

The true drama, however, received birth and perfection from the creative geniuses of Shakespeare, Beaumont and Fletcher, Jonson, and others. Though the stage no sooner began to talk than it grew scurrilous, and plays were thought "Dangerous to Religion, the State, Honesty, and Manners, and also for Infection, in Time of Sickness." Wherefore they were afterwards for some time suppressed. But upon application to the Queen and Council they were again tolerated under the following restrictions: "That no Plays be acted on Sundays at all, nor on any other Holidays till after Evening Prayer. That no playing be in the *Dark*, nor continue and such Time, but the Auditors may return to their Dwellings in London before Sunset, or at least before it be *Dark*." The foregoing is from Stow, and this Act was made in the reign of Elizabeth. The Virgin Queen does not seem to have cared much about this enactment, as we find that on Sunday, the 24th September, 1592, she and her Court attended a play at Oxford.

As Tragedy and Comedy progressed on the English stage, Pantomime, as far as it was associated with the dumb shows in the early English drama, became, little by little, a thing of the past.

We have seen, and traced, from the Creation of this planet, and through succeeding ages, how Pantomime has always flourished; we have seen also how the Interlude gave way to the Comedy; we will now see how this love of light entertainment formulated in this country by the Interlude, and, about the same time, by the Italian Masque Comedy, the progenitor of Pantomime (referring to the whole as a spectacle), and the forerunner in France, also of that other form of light entertainment known as the French Vaudeville, cultivated by Le Sage and other French writers of note.

To go to the bed-rock for our facts, and for the innovation of all this, it is necessary in thought, and perhaps as well in spirit, to journey to Italy.

CHAPTER X. THE ITALIAN MASQUE—THE MASQUE IN ENGLAND

—FIRST APPEARANCE IN THIS COUNTRY OF HARLEQUIN— JOE HAINES AS HARLEQUIN—MARLOWE'S "FAUSTUS"—A CURIOUS PLAY—THE ITALIAN HARLEQUIN—COLLEY CIBBER, PENKETHMAN—SHAKESPEARE'S BURLESQUES OF THE MASQUE—DECLINE OF THE MASQUE.

In Italy the Masque entertainment long held sway, and was a light form of amusement, consisting of Pantomime, music, singing, and dancing, and an adaptation of the *Fabulae Atellanae* of ancient Italy. The performers wore masks, also high-heeled shoes, fitted with brass or iron heels, which jingled as they danced. This ancient custom to present-day stage dancers will doubtless be of interest. Masks, like on the stages of the Greeks and the Romans, were used, hence the title Mask, or Masque, as it is sometimes written both ways. In the days of Elizabeth the custom was also practised in the Elizabethan Masque. The Masquerade and the Masked ball, or *Bal-Masque*, are survivals of this ancient custom.

Crossing the Alps, if the reader will accompany me, the Italian Masque Comedy we find was already known in France in the fifteenth century. In the days of Mary de Medici ballets were introduced, and by the time of Louis XIV. "Opera" (*i.e.*, the Masque) was in full swing in the early part of this reign. On the Spanish stage ballets, with allegorical characters, were known in the sixteenth century; and, in fact, throughout Europe about this age, and some time previously this improvised form of Italian Comedy, and the several characters in it, belonging to the family of Harlequin, had long been familiar subjects.

Returning to England after our little holiday, the Masque in the fifteenth and sixteenth centuries had become very popular. The architect, Inigo Jones, being frequently employed to furnish the decorations with all the magnificence of his invention. At the Courts of Elizabeth, James I., Charles I., and up to the time when all plays were totally suppressed, was it the rage. At the Restoration the Masque was revived again, and here, borrowing the name from the continent, it is called "Opera." In proof of this, in Dryden's work, "Albion and Albanius," 1685, "Opera" is defined as a "poetical tale or picture represented by vocal and instrumental music, and endowed with machines and dances."

The dramatic poet and author, Ben Jonson, collaborated with Inigo Jones, the architect, in devising these Masque plays, Jonson supplying the words, and Jones the scenic effects, the latter being very gorgeous, consisting of "landscapes, mountains, and clouds, which opened to display heathen deities illuminated by variegated coloured lights." Over these Masques or "Operatic" entertainments Jonson and Jones quarrelled, as the former's grievance was that he received no more for his librettos than Jones did for his scenic devices. Ben Jonson thereupon wrote satires upon Inigo Jones, and in one of his squibs appears the satirical line, "Painting and Carpentry are the Soul of Masque." Is not this applicable to many of our present-day Pantomimes, which, as I have just stated in the previous chapter, the Masque was one of the original progenitors?

Inigo Jones and Jonson first collaborated in the "Masque of Blackness," performed at Whitehall on Twelfth Night, 1603. In our money this Masque cost some £10,000. Jones and Jonson's quarrel originated because the poet had, in the "Masque of Chloridia," performed in 1630, prefixed his own name before that of Jones. In consequence of this "rare old Ben" was deprived—through Jones' influence—of employment at Court.

Gifford, in his "Memoirs of Ben Jonson," says that "In poetry, painting, architecture, they (the Masques) have not since been equalled."

"The Masque," continues Gifford, "as it attained its highest degree of excellence, admitted of dialogue, singing and dancing; these were not independent of one another, but combined by the introduction of some ingenious fable into an harmonious whole. When the plan was formed, the aid of the sister-arts was called in; for the essence of the Masque was pomp and glory. Movable scenery of the most costly and splendid kind was lavished on the Masque; the most celebrated masters were employed on the songs and dances; and all that the kingdom afforded of vocal and instrumental excellence was employed to embellish the exhibition. Thus, magnificently constructed, was composed, as Lord Bacon says, for princes, and by princes it was played. Of these Masques, the skill with which their ornaments were designed, and the inexpressible grace with which they were executed appear to have left a vivid impression on the mind of Jonson. His genius awakens at once, and all his faculties attune to sprightliness and pleasure. He makes his appearance like his own Delight, accompanied with Grace, Love, Harmony, Revel, Sport, and Laughter."

In the Masques the Pantomimic dances of the Masquers were known as motions:—

"In curious knot and mazes so

The Spring at first was taught to go;

And Zephyr, when he came to woo

His Flora had his *motions* too;

And thus did Venus learn to lead

The Idalian brawls, and so to tread,

As if the wind, not she did walk,

Nor press'd a flower, nor bow'd a stalk."

Before the arrival of the Italian Masque in England, the Harlequin family were unknown, and, doubtless, Harlequin's first appearance in this country was in consonance with the Masque itself.

Heywood, in a tract, published in 1609, entitled, "*Troia Britannica*," mentions "Zanyes, Pantaloons, Harlakeans, in which the French, but especially the Italians, have been excellent as known in this country."

The earliest record I can find of a Harlequin performing in this country is in the Masque given before Charles I. and his Court on the Sunday evening following Twelfth Night, 1637. An account of this Masque, as well as other information dealing with the Masque entertainments, will be found in my volume, "Stage Whispers," and in the article on theatrical scenery.

In a comedy, written by Ravenscroft, after the Italian manner, Joe Haines, in 1667, donned the motley jacket of Harlequin, and which, in all probability, was the first appearance of Harlequin on the English boards, though not in England, as stated above. In a farce of the audacious Mrs. Aphra Behn's, produced twenty years afterwards, Harlequin and Scaramouch were two of the characters. Mrs. Behn died April 16, 1689, and was buried in the cloisters of Westminster Abbey. To Marlowe's "Faustus," Mountfort added comic scenes to the tragedy, introducing Harlequin and Scaramouch. A Harlequin, Pantaloon, Columbine, and Clown appeared in a curious piece in 1697, entitled, "Novelty; or Every Act a Play." The first act consisted of a pastoral Drama, the second of a Comedy, the third a Masque, the fourth a Tragedy, and the fifth act a Farce.

In Italy the fame of Harlequin was at its zenith at the close of the seventeenth century. In this country in 1687 a Harlequin (Penkethman) appeared in a farce called "The Emperor of the Moon" without a mask. Colley Cibber says of this performance "That when he (Penkethman) first played Harlequin in 'The Emperor of the Moon' several gentlemen (who inadvertently judged by the rules of nature) fancied that a great deal of the drollery, and spirit of his grimace was lost by his wearing that useless, unmeaning mask, therefore insisted that the next time of his acting that part he should play without it. Their desire was accordingly complied with, but alas! in vain—Penkethman was no more Harlequin. His humour was quite disconcerted."

In "The Tempest," Shakespeare introduces a Masque, and also in his "Midsummer Nights' Dream," the play of "Pyramus and Thisbe," performed by the Clowns, is in burlesque of the Masque plays.

In both these two plays of the bard's, and in connection with the Masque plays, we see, from the stage directions in them, how Pantomime formed part of their effective representation.

In out heroding-herod in the way of splendour, showy dresses and expensive machinery, the Masque soon fell into decay; and, as Ben Jonson states, "The glory of all these solemnities had perished like a blaze, and gone out in the beholder's eyes; so short-lived are the bodies of all things in comparison with their souls."

CHAPTER XI. ITALIAN PANTOMIME— RICCOBONI

—BROOM'S "ANTIPODES"—GHERARDI—EXTEMPORAL COMEDIES—SALVATOR ROSA—IMPROMPTU ACTING.

Pantomime in Italy had two distinct features, one a species of buffoonery, termed *Lazzi*, and the other Extemporal or Improvised Comedies.

"*Lazzi*," mentions Riccoboni, in his "*Histoire du Theâtre Italien*," is a term corrupted from the old Tuscan *Lacci*, which signifies a knot, or something that connects. (Both the *Lazzi* and the Extemporal Comedies were all derived from the one original source, that of the Satirical drama of the Greeks, and perpetuated in the *Fabulae Atellanae* or *Laudi Osci* of Italy.)

Riccoboni continues: "These pleasantries, called *Lazzi*, are certain actions by which the performer breaks into the scene, to paint to the eye his emotions of panic or jocularity; but as such gestures are foreign to the business going on, the nicety of the art consists in not interrupting the scene, and connecting the *Lazzi* with it; thus to tie the whole together."

Lazzi is what we might term "bye play," which, by gesture and action, could not detract, but rather added to the effectiveness of the scene in progress.

In Broom's "Antipodes," which was performed at the Salisbury Court Theatre, London, in 1638, a *by-play*, as he calls it, is represented in this comedy—"A word (explains Malone) for the application of which we are indebted to this writer, there being no other term in our language that I know of, which so properly expresses that species of Interlude which we find in our poet's 'Hamlet,' and other pieces."

Riccoboni, in describing some *Lazzi*, says that Harlequin and Scapin being in a famished condition, Scapin, in order to bring their young mistress out, asks Harlequin to groan. Scapin explains to her the reason, and while they are talking, Harlequin is performing his *Lazzi*. This consists of eating an imaginary hatful of cherries, and throwing the stones at Scapin; or catching imaginary flies, and chopping off their wings.

"*Lazzi*," we are told, "although they seem to interrupt the progress of the action, yet in cutting it they slide back into it, and connect or tie the whole."

When Riccoboni and his company first appeared in France, though being unable to speak nothing but Italian, their audiences, though not being able to understand the *words*, yet the performers were such past-masters in the Mimetic Art that their representations were just as intelligible and as expressive as if they had been with words.

Gherardi, in his treatise, "*Theâtre Italien*," speaks of a Scaramouch, who, waiting for his master, Harlequin, seats and plays on the guitar. Suddenly, by Pasquariel, he is thrown into a fright. "It was then," says Gherardi, "that incomparable model of our most eminent actors displayed the miracles of his art; that art which paints the passions in the face, throws them into every gesture, and through a whole scene of frights upon frights, conveys the most powerful expression of ludicrous terror. This man moved all hearts by the simplicity of nature, more than skilful orators can with all the charms of persuasive rhetoric."

The Extemporal Comedies were all improvised, the actors underwent no rehearsal, and, as the name denotes, everything was impromptu. The Scenario, or plot, had just simply the scenes and the characters set forth, and it was then hung in a conspicuous place on the stage; and just in a similar way as the gas or lime light "plots" are affixed in present day theatres, though the Scenarios were not as elaborate as what some of our gas or limelight "plots" are.

Before going on the stage, the Mimes just inspected the Scenario of the *Comedia Del' Arte*, and for the dialogue and action everything depended solely upon their Pantomimic genius.

Disraeli mentions that men of great genius had a passion for performing in these Extemporal Comedies, and, amongst others, the great painter, Salvator Rosa. A favourite character of Rosa's was that of Formica, a Clown of Calabria. Passeri, in his life of Rosa, tells the following anecdote:—

One summer, Salvator Rosa joined a company of young persons, who were curiously addicted to the making of *Comedie all' Improviso*. In the midst of a vineyard they raised a rustic stage, under the direction of one Mussi, who enjoyed some literary reputation, particularly for his sermons preached in Lent.

Their second Comedy was numerously attended, and I went among the rest. I sat on the same bench by good fortune with Cavalier Bernini, Romanelli, and Guido, all well-known persons. Salvator Rosa, who had already made himself a favourite with the Roman people, under the character of Formica, opened with a prologue in company with other actors. He proposed for relieving themselves of the extreme heats and *ennui* that they should make a Comedy, and all agreed. Formica (Rosa) then spoke (in the satirical Venetian dialect) these exact words, which Mr. Disraeli translates as follows:—"I will not, however, that we should make a Comedy like certain persons who cut clothes, and put them on this man's back, and on that man's back; for at last the time comes which shows how much faster went the cut of the shears than the pen of the poet; nor will we have entering on the scene, couriers, brandy sellers, and goatherds, and there stare shy and blockish, which I think worthy the senseless invention of an ass."

Passeri continues: "At this time Bernini had made a Comedy in the Carnival very pungent and biting; and that summer he had one of Castelli's performed in the suburbs, where, to represent the dawn of day, appeared on the stage water-carriers, couriers, and goat-herds, going about—all which is contrary to rule, which allows of no character who is not concerned in the dialogue to mix with the groups. At these words of the Formica, I, who well knew his meaning, instantly glanced my eye at Bernini, to observe his movements; but he, with an artificial carelessness, showed that this 'cut of the shears' did not touch him; and he made no apparent show of being hurt. But Castelli, who was also near, tossing his head and smiling in bitterness, showed clearly that he was hit."

In concluding, Mr. Disraeli observes that: "This Italian story, told with all the poignant relish of these vivacious natives, to whom such a stinging incident was an important event, also shows the personal freedoms taken on these occasions by a man of genius, entirely in the spirit of the ancient Roman *Atellanae* or the Grecian *Satyra*."

Of Extemporal Comedies, Riccoboni mentions that: "This kind of spectacle is peculiar to Italy; one cannot deny that it has graces perfectly its own, and which *written Comedy can never exhibit*. This impromptu mode of acting furnishes opportunities for a perpetual change in the performance, so that the same Scenario repeated still appears a new one: thus one Comedy may become twenty Comedies. *An actor of this description, always supposing an actor of genius, is more vividly affected than one who has coldly got his part by rote. But figure, memory, voice, and even sensibility, are not sufficient for the actor all' improvista; he must be in the habit of cultivating the imagination, pouring forth the flow of expression, and prompt in those flashes which instantly vibrate in the plaudits of an audience*."

Again, Gherardi: "Anyone may learn a part by rote, and do something bad, or indifferent, on another theatre. With us the affair is quite otherwise; and when an Italian actor dies, it is with infinite difficulty that we can supply his place. An Italian actor learns nothing by head; he looks on the subject for a moment before he comes forward on the stage, and entirely depends upon his imagination for the rest. The actor who is accustomed merely to recite what he has been taught is so completely occupied by his memory, that he appears to stand, as it were, unconnected either with the audience or his companions; he is so impatient to deliver himself of the burthen he is carrying that he trembles like a schoolboy, or is as senseless as an echo, *and could never speak if others had not spoken before.* Such a tutored actor among us would be like a paralytic arm to a body: an unserviceable member, only fatiguing the healthy action of the sound parts."

CHAPTER XII. PANTOMIMICAL CHARACTERS

—NEAPOLITAN PANTOMIME—THE HARLEQUIN FAMILY— THE ORIGINAL CHARACTERS IN THE ITALIAN PANTOMIMES—CELEBRATED HARLEQUINS—ITALIAN AND FRENCH HARLEQUINS—A FRENCH VIEW OF THE ENGLISH CLOWN—PIERROTS' ORIGIN—PANTALOON, HOW THE NAME HAS BEEN DERIVED—COLUMBINE—MARIONETTE AND PUPPET SHOWS.

After having shown what the *Lazzi* and Extemporal Comedies were like, let us now turn to the Pantomimical characters associated with their representations.

Every one, observes Mr. Isaac Disraeli, of this grotesque family were the creatures of national genius, chosen by the people for themselves. Italy, both ancient and modern, exhibits a gesticulating people of comedians, and the same comic genius characterised the nation through all its revolutions, as well as the individual through all his fortunes.

The lower classes still betray their aptitude in that vivid humour, where the action is suited to the word—silent gestures sometimes expressing whole sentences. They can tell a story, and even raise the passions, without opening their lips. No nation in modern Europe possesses so keen a relish for the burlesque, insomuch as to show a class of unrivalled poems, which are distinguished by the very title; and perhaps there never was an Italian in a foreign country, however deep in trouble, but would drop all remembrance of his sorrows, should one of his countrymen present himself with the paraphernalia of Punch at the corner of a street. I was acquainted with an Italian, a philosopher and a man of fortune, residing in this country, who found so lively a pleasure in performing Punchinello's little comedy, that, for this purpose, with considerable expense and curiosity, he had his wooden company, in all their costume, sent over from his native place. The shrill squeak of the tin whistle had the same comic effect on him as the notes of the *Ranz des Vaches* have in awakening the tenderness of domestic emotions in the wandering Swiss—the national genius is dramatic. Lady Wortley Montagu when she resided at a villa near Brescia, was applied to by the villagers for leave to erect a theatre in her saloon: they had been accustomed to turn the stables into a playhouse every Carnival. She complied, and, as she tells us, was "Surprised at the beauty of their scenes, though painted by a country painter. The performance was yet more surprising, the actors being all peasants; but the Italians have so natural a genius for comedy, they acted as well as if they had been brought up to nothing else, particularly the Arlechino, who far surpassed any of our English, though only the tailor of our village, and I am assured never saw a play in any other place." Italy is the mother, and the nurse, of the whole Harlequin race.

Hence it is that no scholars in Europe but the most learned Italians, smit by the national genius, could have devoted their vigils to narrate the evolutions of Pantomime, to compile the annals of Harlequin, to unroll the genealogy of Punch, and to discover even the most secret anecdotes of the obscurer branches of that grotesque family, amidst their changeful fortunes, during a period of two thousand years. Nor is this all; princes have ranked them among the Rosciuses; and Harlequins and Scaramouches have been ennobled. Even Harlequins themselves have written elaborate treatises on the almost insurmountable difficulties of their art. I despair to convey the sympathy they have inspired me with to my reader; but every *Tramontane* genius must be informed, that of what he has never seen, he must rest content to be told.

Of the ancient Italian troop we have retained three or four of the characters, while their origin has nearly escaped our recollection; but of the burlesque comedy, the extempore dialogue, the humorous fable, and its peculiar species of comic acting, all has vanished.

Many of the popular pastimes of the Romans unquestionably survived their dominion, for the people will amuse themselves, though their masters may be conquered; and tradition has never proved more faithful than in preserving popular sports. Many of the games of our children were played by Roman boys; the mountebanks, with the dancers and tumblers on their moveable stages, still in our fairs, are Roman; the disorders of the *Bacchanalia*, Italy appears to imitate in her Carnivals. Among these Roman diversions certain comic characters have been transmitted to us, along with some of their characteristics, and their dresses. The speaking Pantomimes and Extemporal Comedies which have delighted the Italians for many centuries, are from this ancient source.

Rich, in his "Companion to the Latin Dictionary," has an excellent illustration of this passage:—"This Art was of very great antiquity, and much practiced by the Greeks and Romans, both on the stage and in the tribune, induced by their habit of addressing large assemblies in the open air, where it would have been impossible for the majority to comprehend what was said without the assistance of some conventional signs, which enabled the speaker to address himself to the eye, as well as the ear of the audience. These were chiefly made by certain positions of the hands and fingers, the meaning of which was universally recognised and familiar to all classes, and the practice itself reduced to a regular system, as it remains at the present time amongst the populace of Naples, who will carry on a long conversation between themselves by mere gesticulation, and without pronouncing a word." That many of these signs are similar to those used by the Ancients, is proved by the same author, who copies from an antique vase a scene which he explains by the action of the hands of the figures, adding, "A common lazzaroni, when shown one of these compositions, will at once explain the purport of the action, which a scholar with all his learning cannot divine." The gesture to signify love, employed by the Ancients and modern Neapolitans, was joining the tips of the thumb and forefinger of the left hand; an imputation or asseveration by holding forth the right hand; a denial by raising the same hand, extending the fingers. In mediaeval works of art, a particular attitude of the fingers is adopted to exhibit malicious hate: it is done by crossing the forefinger of each hand, and is generally seen in figures of Herod or Judas Iscariot.

Down to the fifteenth century there is not much known of the family of Harlequin, with the exception, perhaps, that the name Zany became more widely distributed into such as Drolls, Clowns, Pantaloons, Punches, Scaramouches, and the like. In the Italian Comedy, of purely native growth, the original characters were Pantaloon, a Venetian Merchant; Dottore, a Bolognese physician; Spavento, a Neapolitan braggart; Pulcinello, a wag of Apalia; Giangurgoto and Corviello, two Clowns of Cala-simpleton; and Arlechino, a blundering servant of Bergamo.

The latter The Harlequin of the Italian theatre, has passed through, mentions Mr. Disraeli, all the vicissitudes of fortune. At first (as we have seen) he was a true representative of the ancient Mime; but, during the fourteenth and fifteenth centuries, he degenerated into a booby and a gourmand, the perpetual butt for a sharp-witted fellow, his companion, Brighella, the knife and the whetstone. Harlequin, however, under the reforming hand of Goldoni, became, in after years, a child of nature, and the delight of his country; and he has commemorated the historical character of the great Harlequin Sacchi. It may serve the reader to correct his notions of one, from the absurd pretender with us who has usurped the title. "Sacchi possessed a lively and brilliant imagination. While other Harlequins merely repeated themselves, Sacchi, who always adhered to the essence of the play, contrived to give an air of freshness to the piece by his new sallies and unexpected repartees. His comic traits and his jests were neither taken from the language of the lower orders, nor that of the comedians. He levied contributions on comic authors, on poets, orators, and philosophers; and in his impromptus they often discovered the thoughts of Seneca, Cicero, or Montaigne. He possessed the art of appropriating the remains of these great men to himself, and allying them to the simplicity of the blockhead; so that the same proposition which was admired in a serious author, became highly ridiculous in the mouth of this excellent actor." In France Harlequin was improved into a wit, and even converted into a moralist; he is the graceful hero of Florian's charming compositions, which please even in the closet. "This imaginary being, invented by the Italians, and adopted by the French," says the ingenious Goldoni, "has the exclusive right of uniting *naiveté* with *finesse*, and no one ever surpassed Florian in the delineation of this amphibious character. He has even contrived to impart sentiment, passion, and morality to his pieces." Harlequin must be modelled as a national character, the creature of manners; and thus the history of such a Harlequin might be that of the age and of the people, whose genius he ought to represent.

The history of a people is often detected in their popular amusements; one of these Italian Pantomimic characters shows this. They had a *Capitan*, who probably originated in the *Miles gloriosus* of Plautus; a brother, at least, of our Ancient Pistol and Bobadil. The ludicrous names of this military poltroon were Spavento (Horrid fright), Spezza-fer (Shiver-spear), and a tremendous recreant was Captain Spavento de Val inferno. When Charles V. entered Italy, a Spanish Captain was introduced; a dreadful man he was too, if we are to be frightened by names: Sangre e Fuego! and Matamoro! His business was to deal in Spanish rhodomontades, to kick out the native Italian Capitan, in compliment to the Spaniards, and then to take a quiet caning from Harlequin, in compliment to themselves. When the Spaniards lost their influence in Italy, the Spanish Captain was turned into Scaramouch, who still wore the Spanish dress, and was perpetually in a panic. The Italians could only avenge themselves on the Spaniards in Pantomime! On the same principle the gown of Pantaloon over his red waistcoat and breeches, commemorates a circumstance in Venetian history expressive of the popular feeling.

The characters of the Italian Pantomime became so numerous, that every dramatic subject was easily furnished with the necessary personages of comedy. That loquacious pedant, the Dottore, was taken from the lawyers and the physicians, babbling false Latin in the dialect of learned Bologna. Scapin was a livery servant, who spoke the dialect of Bergamo, a province proverbially abounding with rank intriguing knaves, who, like the slaves in Plautus and Terence, were always on the watch to further any wickedness; while Calabria furnished the booby Giangurgello with his grotesque nose. Molière, it has been ascertained, discovered in the Italian theatre at Paris his "*Medecin malgre Lui*," his "*Etourdi*," his "*L'Avare*," and his "*Scapin*." Milan offered a pimp in Brighella; Florence, an ape of fashion in Gelsomino. These and other Pantomimic characters, and some ludicrous ones, as the Tartaglia, a spectacled dotard, a stammerer, and usually in a passion, had been gradually introduced by the inventive powers of an actor of genius, to call forth his own peculiar talents.

The Pantomimes, or, as they have been described, the continual Masquerades, of Ruzzante, with all these diversified personages, talking and acting, formed, in truth, a burlesque comedy. Some of the finest geniuses of Italy became the votaries of Harlequin; and the Italian Pantomime may be said to form a school of its own. The invention of Ruzzante was one capable of perpetual novelty. Many of these actors have been chronicled either for the invention of some comic character, or for their true imitation of nature in performing some favourite one. One, already immortalised by having lost his real name in that of Captain Matamoros, by whose inimitable humours he became the most popular man in Italy, invented the Neapolitan Pullicinello; while another, by deeper study, added new graces to another burlesque rival. One Constantini invented the character of Mezetin, as the Narcissus of Pantomime. He acted without a mask, to charm by the beautiful play of his countenance, and display the graces of his figure; the floating drapery of his fanciful dress could be arranged by the changeable humour of the wearer. Crowds followed him in the streets, and a King of Poland ennobled him. The Wit and Harlequin Dominic sometimes dined at the table of Louis XIV.—Tiberio Florillo, who invented the character of Scaramouch, had been the amusing companion of the boyhood of Louis XIV.; and from him Molière learnt much, as appears by the verses under his portrait:—

Cet illustre comédien

De son art traça la carrière:

Il fut le maître de Molière,

Et la Nature fut le sien.

The last lines of an epitaph on one of these Pantomimic actors may be applied to many of them during their flourishing period:—

Toute sa vie il a fait rire;

Il a fait pleurer a sa mort.

Several of these admirable actors were literary men, who have written on their art, and shown that it was one. The Harlequin Cecchini composed the most ancient treatise on this subject, and was ennobled by the Emperor Matthias; and Nicholas Barbieri, for his excellent acting called the Beltrame, a Milanese simpleton, in his treatise on comedy, tells us that he was honoured by the conversation of Louis XIII., and rewarded with fortune.

A sketch of Harlequin's original part is worth recording. "He is a mixture of wit, simplicity, ignorance, and grace, he is a half made up man, a great child with gleams of reason and intelligence, and all his mistakes and blunders have something arch about them. The true mode of representing him is to give him suppleness, agility, the playfulness of a kitten with a certain coarseness of exterior, which renders his actions more absurd. His part is that of a faithful valet; greedy; always in love; always in trouble, either on his own or his master's account; afflicted and consoled as easily as a child, and whose grief is as amusing as his joy."

His costume consisted of a jacket fastened in front with loose ribbons, and pantaloons of wide dimensions, patched with various coloured pieces of cloth sewn on in any fashion. His beard was worn straight, and of a black colour; on his face he had a half black mask and in his belt of untanned leather he carried a wooden sword.

In Italy there were many varieties of Harlequin, the most notable being Trivelin, and Truffaldin. The dress of the former, instead of the patches symmetrically arranged, had triangular patches along the seams, and suns and moons only for patches. He wore the soft hat and hare's foot, but did not carry the wooden sword. The hare's foot denoting speed, has in all probability its origin in the winged cap of the god Mercury.

Truffaldin is a species of Harlequin, who first appeared about 1530. He represented (*truffa*, the villain) a sneaking kind of knave, and in the middle of the seventeenth century this character was very popular.

In France, about 1660, Cardinal Mazarin invited one Joseph Dominique Biancolelli, to come to Paris to give entertainments. Shortly after his arrival Biancolelli gave quite a new reading to the character of Arlechino, as he made him not only a wit and punster, but also a bit of a philosopher. Biancolelli's improvements did not end here, as he turned his attention to the dress of Arlechino, which was now made of finer and better quality, whilst the parti-coloured patches were made more artistic and attractive. On the death of Lolatelli, who, in his lifetime, had played a kind of Arlechino part, Biancolelli succeeded him, and soon sprang into prominence, and acquired a great artistic reputation. Whilst dancing before Louis XV. Biancolelli contracted a cold, which set up inflammation of the lungs, causing his death. His companions, at the theatre in which he performed, to mark the sense of their great grief, closed the theatre for a month. Biancolelli died in 1688.

As Arlechino, Biancolelli was succeeded by his son, Pierre, who played under the name of Dominique.

A Tuscan, named Gherardi, who had obtained celebrity as a singer, was the next successful French Harlequin. In consequence of a fall Gherardi met his death, in the year 1700.

Nearly a couple of decades afterwards, in 1716, Thomassin made his appearance as Harlequin, in pieces written for him by Marivaux, such as "*Le Prince Travesti*," "*La Surprise de l'Amour*," and in which he appeared with great success. So daring were Thomassin's tricks, and in such popularity was he held, that, fearful of losing their favourite like Gherardi, he was obliged to discontinue them.

Another competitor now arose to take the crown from Thomassin, and in the person of one Carlo Bertinazzi, commonly called Carlin. Our actor, Garrick, was an admirer of this famous Mime. Of Carlin, M. Sand speaks:—"Like most clever buffoons, he had a very melancholy disposition, and, as with Dominique, his gaiety was what the English term humour. It belonged to his mind, and not to his temperament." Carlin also wrote a book entitled, "*Les Metamorphosis d'Arlequin*." In 1783 Carlin died, and his place in the favour of the public was filled by Galinetti.

The French view of the English Clown is interesting: "The English clown (whose nearest representative on the French stage is Pierrot) is an odd and fantastical being. The Florentine Stentorella alone resembles him in his jests and tricks. His strange dress seems to have been taken from the American Indians. It consists of a white, red, yellow, and green net work, ornamented with diamond-shaped pieces of stuff of various colours. His face is floured, and streaked with paint a deep carmine; the forehead is prolonged to the top of the head, which is covered with a red wig, from the centre of which a little stiff tail points to the sky. His manners are no less singular than his costume. He is not dumb, like our Pierrot, but, on the contrary, he sustains an animated and witty conversation; he is also an acrobat, and very expert in feats of strength."

M. Blandelaire gives a more poetical description: "The English Pierrot is not a person as pale as the moon, mysterious as silent, straight and long, like the gallows to whom we have been accustomed in Deburean. The English Pierrot enters like the tempest, and tumbles like a parcel; his laugh resembles joyous thunder. He is short and fat; his face is floured and streaked with paint; he has a great patch of red on each cheek; his mouth is enlarged by prolongation of the lips by means of two red bands, so that when he laughs his mouth appears to open from ear to ear."

The Pierrots—not only in France, but on the Continent generally—took all the characteristics of the Zanys, Bertoldo, Paggliaccio, Gros, Giullaume, Pedrolino, Gilles, Corviello, and Peppe Nappa, of the Italian Comedy, and all owing at least their original conception to the theatres of the Greeks, and the Romans. On the Italian stage there was not a principal Clown like in England, the foremost place being occupied by Arlechino. The four principal masked characters of the Italian *Comedia del' Arte* in Venice consisted of Tartaglia (a stammerer), Truffildino, Brighella (a representative of orators and public personages), and Pantaloon (a native of Venice). The name of Pantaloon is derived from *planta-leone* (*plante-lion*—he planted the lion). The probable meaning of it in this particular is that the Venetian merchants, it is said, in boasting of their conquests set up their standard—the Venetian standard being the lion of St. Mark—on various islands in the Mediterranean, and from which they were nicknamed, it is said, "plant lion." A more probable derivation of the word is that the ancient patron saint of Venice is San Pantaleone. St. Pantaleone's day is July 27. He was martyred A.D. 303. In "Childe Harold," Lord Byron, in Canto IV., stanza 14, has that "The Venetian name of Pantaleone is her very by-word."

Pantaloon has been, at various times, husband, father, and widower. Sometimes he is rich, then poor, and occasionally a spendthrift. The dress that he wore consisted of tight red breeches, rather short, a long black robe, red stockings and waistcoat, a little woollen skull-cap and slippers.

When the Venetian republic lost Negropont mourning generally was adopted, and Pantaloon adopted it with the rest, and on the Continent mourning has, I believe, formed a component part of Pantaloon's dress ever since.

In 1750 Darbes, in Italy, was one of the best Pantaloons. Darbes, on one occasion, ventured to play this character in one of Goldoni characters, without a mask, and which, we are told, was a failure. A similar attempt was made on the English stage, which I have previously referred to.

Mention has been previously made of females appearing on the stage during the Grecian and Roman periods. From this, however, there arose on the Italian stage, in after years, the *Servetta* or *Fantesca*, a kind of waiting maid, or "accomplished companion" part, and called later, in France, *Soubrette*, and the origin of which, in all probability, can be traced to the *Mimas* of *Pantomimus*.

In the sixteenth century mention is made of a troupe of performers known as *Amorosos* or *Innamortos*, appearing in Italy. Those who only appeared in the female parts were known as Colombina, Oliva, Fianetta, Pasquella, and Nespella. Columbina's part, the "accomplished companion," like the *Vita* of the Indian Drama, was sometimes that of mistress, and sometimes that of maid. Up to 1560 women were unknown on the Italian stage. In England just one hundred years later.

Three generations of the family of Biancolelli, the Harlequin, grandmother, grand-daughter, and great grand-daughter appeared as Columbines in France. The most talented was Catherine, the daughter of Dominique, and she made her *debut* in 1683, in "*Arlequin Protée*," with great success.

About 1695, Columbine appeared in a parti-coloured gown like a female Harlequin, and in the piece "*Le Retour de la foie de Besons*," acted at the Comedie Italiene. As the innovation was much liked, the part of Columbine came to be dressed like the Harlequin. The Columbine dressed in short muslin skirts is a creation of modern times. In the French Comedies Columbine was often Harlequin's wife, but she never had the powers of a magical wand.

In the old form of Pantomime there were many other personages in these dumb shows which we never had in the English Pantomimes. To note a few of them:—The Captain, a bragging swash-buckler; the Apothecary, a half-starved individual with a red nose; and a female *soubrette*, who acted for her mistress, Columbine, similar duties as what Clown performed as valet for his master. The Doctor brought at first on the stage in 1560, was supposed to be a lawyer or a physician. From 1560 his dress was that of a professor's, a short, black tunic, stockings, and a black mask covering the forehead and nose. Another, Façanappa, had a long parrot nose, surmounted by a pair of green spectacles, a flat hat, with a broad brim, a waistcoat covered with tinsel, and a long white coat with large pockets. Like the Clown of our early English plays, and like his ancestors, the *Atellans* and *Mimes*, he had the privilege of making allusions from the stage, in what, I suppose, were something like the Interludes. Il Barone is another variety. He was a Sicilian lord, deceived by his daughter, and also duped by his valets. "*Il Barone*" was a favourite subject for another form of "Miming," that of the wooden figures called Marionettes.

Marionette entertainments were known both to the Greeks and the Romans. The adventures of "*Don Juan*" and "*Don Giovanni*," of the Italian Opera, in all probability sprang originally from the adventures of Punch in the puppet shows.

Puppet shows introduced into France (*temp*. Charles IX.) from Italy, where they were and are still known as *Fantoccini*, by Marion—hence their name—and then into this country, are mentioned by Shakespeare, Pepys, Jonson, Swift, and the Essayists.

Puppet shows, in this country, were formerly known as "Motions." Shakespeare's Antolycus frequented fairs and the like, and he also composed a "Motion" of "The Prodigal Son." Mystery plays were also represented by puppets.

In England, especially at Bartholomew Fair, they were always very popular, and the chief survivor of this form of "dumb show" is "Mr. Punch" of our streets, whose ancient history I have briefly mentioned in another chapter, but not that of "Mrs. Punch," on whose history I am unable— however so brief—to throw any light.

Let us now, dear reader, return to England, and trace in this country something more of the History of Pantomime, and for which we will now open another chapter.

CHAPTER XIII. ITALIAN SCENARIOS AND ENGLISH "PLATTS"—PANTALOON

—TARLETON, THE CLOWN—EXTEMPORAL COMEDY—THE POET MILTON—BEN JONSON—THE COMMONWEALTH—"A REIGN OF DRAMATIC TERROR"—ROBERT COX AND HIS "HUMOURS" AND "DROLLERIES"—THE RESTORATION.

It has been thought that our dramatic poet, Massinger, drew upon the Italian Comedy for the humour of some of his plays. That there was some form of intercourse between the English and Italian stage is shown by the discovery of one of the Italian Scenarios, or "Platts," as we know them, at Dulwich College, which discovery Steevens describes as "a mysterious fragment of ancient stage direction, and of a species of dramatic entertainment which no memorial is preserved in any annals of the English stage." The "Platt," written in a large hand, "And containing directions, was thought to have been affixed near the prompter's stand, and it has even an oblong hole in its centre to admit of being suspended on a wooden peg (Disraeli). On it, and in a familiar way, appear the names of the players, such as: Pigg, White and Black, Dick and Sam, Little Will Barne, Jack Gregory, and the Red-faced fellow."

A "Platt" of the "Seven Deadly Sinnes," supposed to have been written by Dick Tarleton, the famous Clown, is preserved, I believe, in Dulwich College. It consists of a pasteboard fifteen inches high, and nine in breadth, and on it is written, in two columns, the following:—

"A tent being placed on the stage for Henry the Sixth; he in it asleep. To him the lieutenant, and a pursuivant (R. Cowley, Jo. Duke), and one warder (R. Pallant). To them Pride, Gluttony, Wrath, and Covetousness at one door; at another door Envy, Sloth, and Lechery. The three put back the four, and so *exeunt.*

"Henry awaking, enter a keeper (J. Sinclair), to him a servant (T. Belt), to him Lidgate and the keeper. *Exit*, then enter again—then Envy passeth over the stage. Lidgate speaks."

These "Platts" were, in all probability, one of the first written forms of Pantomimic entertainments known in England, and borrowed, as mentioned, from the Scenarios of the Italians. That form of home amusement well-known in family circles, "Acting Charades," may be likened to them.

To get all the information that we can obtain of the "Platts," I am sure I cannot do better than quote the words of Mr. Isaac Disraeli, well assured that they will be more acceptable than any I can make.

Some of these "Platts" are on solemn subjects, like the tragic Pantomimes; and in some appear "Pantaloon, and his man Peascod, with *spectacles.*" Steevens observes, that he met with no earlier example of the appearance of Pantaloon, as a specific character on our stage; and that this direction concerning "the spectacles" cannot fail to remind the reader of a celebrated passage in "As you like it." (Scene 6, Act II.).

... "The sixth age shifts

Into the lean and slippered pantaloon;

With spectacles on nose, and pouch on side;

His youthful hose well saved, a world too wide

For his shrunk shank; and his big manly voice,

Turning again toward childish treble, pipes

And whistles in his sound."

Perhaps, he adds, Shakespeare alludes to this personage, as habited in his own time. The old age of Pantaloon is marked by his leanness, and his spectacles and his slippers. He always runs after Harlequin, but cannot catch him; as he runs in slippers and without spectacles, is liable to pass him by without seeing him. Can we doubt that this Pantaloon had come from the Italian theatre, after what we have already said? Does not this confirm the conjecture, that there existed an intercourse between the Italian theatre and our own? Further, Tarleton, the comedian, celebrated for his "Extemporal wit," was the writer or inventor of one of these "Platts." Stow records of one of our actors that "he had a quick, delicate, refined *Extemporal wit*." And Howes, the continuator of Stow's Chronicles of another, that "he had a wondrous, plentiful, pleasant, *Extemporal* wit."

Praiseworthy reference is also made of Tarleton in "Kinde-Hart's Dream," 4to., published in 1592. In 1611 a book was published entitled "Tarleton's Jeasts." Tarleton was so celebrated in his time that his portrait was hung out as a sign for alehouses. "To sit with Tarleton on an ale-post's signe," observes Bishop Hall in his satires. Oldys, in his M.S. notes, mentions that "There is an alehouse sign of a tabor and pipe man, with the name of Tarleton under it, in the borough of Southwark, and it was taken from the print before the old 4to. book of 'Tarleton's Jeasts;' and Lord Oxford had a portrait of him with his tabor and pipe, which was probably taken from the pamphlet called 'Tarleton's Jeasts,' on the title page of which there is a wooden plate of

Tarleton, at full length in his Clown's dress, playing on his pipe with one hand, and beating his drum with the other."

These actors then (continues Mr. Disraeli), who were in the habit of exercising their impromptus, resembled those who performed in the unwritten comedies of the Italians. Gabriel Harvey, the Aristarchus of the day, compliments Tarleton for having brought forward a *new species of dramatic exhibition*. If this compliment paid to Tarleton merely alludes to his dexterity at *extemporaneous wit* in the character of the *Clown*, as my friend Mr. Douce thinks, this would be sufficient to show that he was attempting to introduce on our stage the Extemporal Comedy of the Italians, which Gabriel Harvey distinguishes as "a new species." As for these "Platts," which I shall not venture to call "Scenarios," they surprise by their bareness, conveying no notion of the piece itself, though quite sufficient for the actors. They consist of mere exits and entrances of the actors, and often the real names of the actors are familiarly mixed with those of the *dramatis personae*. Steevens has justly observed, however, on these skeletons, that although "The drift of these dramatic pieces cannot be collected from the mere outlines before us, yet we must not charge them with absurdity. Even the scenes of Shakespeare would have worn as unpromising an aspect, had their skeletons only been discovered." The printed *Scenarios* of the Italian theatre were not more intelligible; exhibiting only the *hints* for scenes.

Thus, I think, we have sufficient evidence of an intercourse subsisting between the English and Italian theatres, not hitherto suspected; and I find an allusion to these Italian Pantomimes, by the great town-wit Tom Nash, in his "Pierce Pennilesse," which shows that he was well acquainted with their nature. He, indeed, exults over them, observing that our plays are "honourable and full of gallant resolution, not consisting, like theirs, of Pantaloon, a Zany, and a w——e (alluding to the women actors of the Italian stage); but of emperors, kings, and princes." My conviction is still confirmed, when I find that Stephen Gosson wrote the comedy of "Captain Mario;" it has not been printed, but "Captain Mario" is one of the Italian characters.

Even at a later period, the influence of these performances reached the greatest name in the English Parnassus. One of the great actors and authors of these pieces, who published eighteen of these irregular productions, was Andreini, whose name must have the honour of being associated with Milton's, for it was his comedy or opera which threw the first spark of the "Paradise Lost" into the soul of the epic poet—a circumstance which will hardly be questioned by those who have examined the different schemes and allegorical personages of the first projected drama of "Paradise Lost": nor was Andreini, as well as many others of this race of Italian dramatists, inferior poets. The Adamo of Andreini was a personage sufficiently original and poetical to serve as the model of the Adam of Milton. The youthful English poet, at its representation, carried it away in his mind. Wit, indeed, is a great traveller; and thus also the "Empiric" of Massinger might have reached us from the Bolognese Dottore.

The late Mr. Hole, the ingenious writer on the "Arabian Nights," observed to me that Molière, it must be presumed, never read Fletcher's plays, yet his "*Bourgeois Gentilhomme*," and the other's "Noble Gentleman," bear in some instances a great resemblance. Both may have been drawn from the same Italian source of comedy which I have here indicated.

Many years after this article was written, appeared "The History of English Dramatic Poetry," by Mr. Collier. That very laborious investigator has an article on "Extemporal Plays and Plots," iii., 393. The nature of these "Platts" or "Plots," he observes, "Our theatrical antiquaries have not explained." The truth is that they never suspected their origin in the Italian "Scenarios." My conjectures are amply confirmed by Mr. Collier's notices of the intercourse of our players with the Italian actors. Whetstone's Heptameron, in

1582, mentions "The comedians of Ravenna, who are not *tied to any written device.*" In Kyd's Spanish Tragedy the Extemporal Art is described:—

The Italian tragedians were so sharp of wit,

That in one hour of meditation

They would perform anything in action.

These Extemporal plays were witnessed much nearer than in Italy—at the *Theâtre des Italiens* at Paris—for one of the characters replies:—

I have seen the like,

In Paris, among the French tragedians.

Ben Jonson has mentioned the Italian "Extemporal Plays," in his "Case is Altered"; and an Italian *commediante* and his company were in London in 1578, who probably let our players into many a secret.

Evil times, with the advent of the Commonwealth, soon fell upon our theatres, and when they, as well as plays, were suppressed by order of the Puritan Parliament, some of the actors followed the Royalist cause (we do not hear of any taking the side of the Parliament), and lost their lives fighting for the king. Others attempted to enact plays in secret, but these performances more often than not, caused the actors incarceration in some prison. At Holland House, in Kensington, many of these secret performances, by the aid of bribery, took place. To give timely warning of the performances Mr. Wright, in his "*Historia Histronica*," mentions that "Alexander Goff, the woman-actor, was the jackal to give notice of time and place to the lovers of the drama."

All this however, could not, and would not, keep the spirit of the drama alive. The theatres were, we know, totally suppressed, "so there might be no more plaies acted." Play-goers there were, as I have shown, but they never knew when, in witnessing a performance, they might be seized by the military, to be fined or imprisoned, or perhaps both. A more lengthy reign of "Dramatic Terror" than what we had at this period, would, in all probability, have left us little or no trace of the Drama of this country. But a saviour was at hand, and that was Pantomime.

Pantomime, as previously stated, kept alive for ages, after the downfall of the Roman Empire, the Dramatic Art, and during the Commonwealth of this country, it practically did the same for us.

Owing to the exigences of the times, one Robert Cox, an actor of considerable genius, after the fashion of the Extemporal Comedies of Italy, invented a series of dramatic exhibitions at the Red Bull Theatre (where the first English actress made her appearance December 8, 1660) and elsewhere, under the guise of rope-dancing, a number of comic scenes from Shakespeare, Shirley, Marston, Beaumont, and Fletcher, and others. Cox's exhibitions, known as "Humours" or "Drolleries," were collected by Marsh, and reprinted (1672) by Francis Kirkman, the author and book-seller. This collection is entitled "The Wits, or Sport upon Sport, in select pieces of Drollery, digested into scenes by way of dialogue. Together with variety of Humours of several nations fitted for the pleasure and content of all persons, either in Court, City, Country, or Camp."

Of these "Humours" Kirkman observes, "As meanly as you may now think of these Drolls, they were then acted by the best comedians; and, I may say, by some that then exceeded all now living; the incomparable Robert Cox, who was not only the principal actor, but also the contriver and author of most of these farces. How I have heard him cried up for his John Swabber, and Simpleton the Smith; in which he being to appear with a large piece of bread and butter, I have frequently known several of the female spectators and auditors to long for it; and once that well-known natural, Jack Adams of Clerkenwell, seeing him with bread and butter on the stage, and knowing him, cried out, 'Cuz! Cuz! give me some!' to the great pleasure of the audience. And so naturally did he act the smith's part, that being at a fair in a country town, and that farce being presented the only master-smith of the town came to him, saying, 'Well, although your father speaks so ill of you, yet when the fair is done, if you will come and work with me, I will give you twelve pence a week more than I give any other journeyman.' Thus was he taken for a smith bred, that was, indeed, as much of any trade."

With the death of the Lord Protector, Cromwell, "The merry rattle of Monk's drums coming up the Gray's Inn Road, welcomed by thousands of dusty spectators," the return of Charles II., 1660, and though Charles was more a lover of the stage than of the drama, the theatre again recovered its credit, and to vigorously flourish once more.

CHAPTER XIV. INTRODUCTION OF PANTOMIMES TO THE ENGLISH STAGE

—WEAVER'S "HISTORY OF THE MIMES AND PANTOMIMES"—WEAVER'S PANTOMIMES—THE PREJUDICE AGAINST PANTOMIMES—BOOTH'S COUNSEL.

The year 1702 marks the appearance of the first Pantomime introduced to the English stage, written by John Weaver, a friend of Addison and Steele's, and entitled "Tavern Bilkers." It was produced at Drury Lane.

The author was by profession a dancing-master; his name is not to be found in any biographical dictionary, yet, it is evident that the "little dapper, cheerful man" had brains in his head as well as talent in his heels.

John Weaver was the son of a Mr. Weaver, whom the Duke of Ormond, the Chancellor of Oxford, licensed in 1676 to exercise the profession of a dancing-master within the university. The date of his birth is unknown, but we first hear of him as stage-managing the production of his own Pantomime at Drury Lane, 1702, an entertainment which he described as one of "dancing, action, and motion." The latter would appear to have been a failure, as in his "History of the Mimes and Pantomimes," published in 1728, Weaver states that his next attempt on similar lines did not take place until many years afterwards—not until the year 1716, in fact. In 1716 Weaver was back in London producing two burlesque Pantomimes, "The Loves of Mars and Venus," and "Perseus and Andromeda." At Drury Lane, in the following year, "Orpheus and Eurydice," and "Harlequin Turn'd Judge," was produced, and "Cupid and Bacchus" in 1719. Weaver also wrote many treatises on dancing, some of which were highly commended by Steele.

Another Pantomime of Weaver's was "The Judgment of Paris"—date uncertain—performed by the author's pupils "in the great room over the Market-house," Shrewsbury—in which town he had taken up his residence—in the year 1750. John Weaver died September 28th, 1760, and was buried at St. Chads, Shrewsbury.

The mention above of "Perseus and Andromeda" calls to mind that there were several pieces of this name. One of them was severely commented on in "The Grub-Street Journal" of April 8, 1731. Its title was:—"Perseus and Andromeda; or the Flying Lovers, in five Interludes, three serious and two comic. The serious composed by Monsieur Roger, the comic by John Weaver, dancing-masters."

It is only just to assign to Weaver the entire credit of being the first to introduce Pantomimes on the English stage, though the author's original bent was "scenical dancing," or ballet dancing, by representations of historical incidents with graceful motion. In his "History of Pantomimes" the author is careful to distinguish between those entertainments where "Grin and grimace usurp the passions and affections of the mind," and those where "A nice address and management of the passions take up the thoughts of the performer." "Spectators," says Weaver, in 1730, or thereabouts, "are now so pandering away their applause on interpolations of pseudo-players, merry Andrews, tumblers, and rope dancers; and are but rarely touched with, or encourage a natural player or just Pantomime."

It was, however, left to John Rich to place Pantomime on a firm footing. Before dealing with Rich and his Pantomimes, which I shall treat of in the next chapter, it is appropriate here to note how Pantomimes generally came to be introduced on the English stage.

Colley Cibber mentions:—About this time the patentee (Rich) having very near finished his house in Lincoln's Inn Fields, began to think of forming a new company; and, in the meantime, found it necessary to apply for leave to employ them. By the weak defence he had always made against the several attacks upon his interests, and former Government of the theatre (Drury Lane), it might be a question, if his house had been ready, in the Queen's (Anne) time, whether he would then have had the spirit to ask, or interest enough to obtain leave to use it; but in the following reign, as it did not appear he had done anything to forfeit the right of his patent, he prevailed with Mr. Craggs, the younger, to lay his case before the king, which he did in so effectual a manner that (as Mr. Craggs himself told me) his Majesty was pleased to say upon it, "That he remembered when he had been in England before, in King Charles's time, there had been two theatres in London; and as the patent seemed to be a lawful grant, he saw no reason why two play-houses might not be continued."

The suspension of the patent being thus taken off, the younger multitude seemed to call aloud for two play-houses! Many desired another, from the common notion, that two would always create emulation, in the actors. Others too were as eager for them, from the natural ill-will that follows the fortunate or prosperous in any undertaking. Of this low malevolence we had, now and then, remarkable instances; we had been forced to dismiss an audience of a hundred and fifty pounds, from a disturbance spirited up, by obscure people, who never gave any better reason for it than that it was their fancy to support the idle complaint of one rival actress against another, in their several pretensions to the chief part in a new tragedy. But as this tumult seemed only to be the wantonness of English liberty, I shall not presume to lay any further censure upon it.

Now, notwithstanding this public desire of re-establishing two houses; and though I have allowed the former actors greatly our superiors; and the managers I am speaking of not to have been without their private errors, yet under all these disadvantages, it is certain, the stage, for twenty years before this time, had never been in so flourishing a condition.

But, in what I have said, I would not be understood to be an advocate for two play-houses; for we shall soon find that two sets of actors, tolerated in the same place, have constantly ended in the corruption of the theatre; of which the auxiliary entertainments, that have so barbarously supplied the defects of weak action, have, for some years past, been a flagrant instance; it may not, therefore, be here improper to shew how our childish Pantomimes first came to take so gross a possession of the stage.

I have upon several occasions, already observed, that when one company is too hard for another, the lower in reputation has always been forced to exhibit fine newfangled foppery, to draw the multitude after them; of these expedients, singing and dancing had formerly been most effectual; but, at the time I am speaking of, our English music had been so discountenanced since the taste of Italian Operas prevailed, that it was to no purpose to pretend to it. Dancing, therefore, was now the only weight, in the opposite scale, and as the new theatre sometimes found their account in it, it could not be safe for us wholly to neglect it.

Cibber's antagonistical views towards Pantomime were shared, as we shall see, by a good many others.

Booth, however, a greater actor than Cibber, and a tragedian to boot, took a more business-like view of the proceedings, thinking thin houses the greatest indignity the stage could suffer. "Men of taste and judgment (said he) must necessarily form but a small proportion of the spectators at a theatre, and if a greater number of people were enticed to sit out a play because a Pantomime was tacked to it, the Pantomime did good service to all concerned. Besides, if people of position and taste could, if so minded, leave before the nonsense commenced—an opportunity they do not seem to have embraced since Booth reminded the opponents of Pantomime how Italian opera had drawn the nobility and gentry away from the play-houses, as appeared by the melancholy testimony of their receipts, until Pantomime came to the rescue when pit and gallery were better filled, and the boxes too put on a nobler appearance."

CHAPTER XV. JOHN RICH AND HIS PANTOMIMES—RICH'S MIMING—-GARRICK, WALPOLE, FOOTE—ANECDOTES OF RICH—POPE

—THE DANCE OF INFERNALS IN "HARLEQUIN SORCERER"—DRURY LANE—COLLEY CIBBER—HENRY FIELDING, THE NOVELIST—CONTEMPORARY WRITERS' OPINION OF PANTOMIME—WOODWARD, THE HARLEQUIN—THE MEANING OF THE WORD ACTOR—HARLEQUINS—"DR. FAUSTUS," A DESCRIPTION—WILLIAM RUFUS CHETWOOD—ACCIDENTS—VANDERMERE, THE HARLEQUIN—"ORPHEUS AND EURYDICE" AT COVENT GARDEN—A DESCRIPTION—SAM. HOOLE, THE MACHINIST—PREJUDICE AGAINST PANTOMIME—MRS. OLDFIELD—ROBERT WILKS—MACKLIN—RIOT AT LINCOLN'S INN FIELDS THEATRE—DEATH OF RICH.

It was in 1717 that Rich devised this new form of entertainment, though it was not till 1724, when "The Necromancer, or History of Dr. Faustus" was produced by Rich, which took the town by storm, that Pantomime became such a rage. It has been stated that what induced Rich to turn his attention to Pantomime was the bringing over of a German, named Swartz, who had two performing dogs that could dance. They were engaged at £10 a night; and brought full houses. However, be this as it may, in the "Daily Courant," of December 20, 1717, we find him, advertising for his "Italian Mimic Scenes"—as he, for long enough, so termed his Pantomimes—as follows:—

"Harlequin Executed: a new Italian Mimic Scene between a

Scaramouch, a Harlequin, a Country Farmer, his Wife, and

others."

Of Rich and his early Pantomimes, Davies observes:—

John Rich was the son of Christopher Rich, formerly patentee of Drury Lane Theatre, and he imbibed from his father a *dislike of people with whom he was obliged to live and converse*. His father wished to acquire wealth by French dancers and Italian singers, than by the united skill of the most accomplished comedians. The son inherited the same taste, and when he came into the patent, with his brother Christopher, of Drury Lane, and after having ineffectually tried his talent for acting in the part of the Earl of Essex, and other important characters, he applied himself to the study of Pantomimical representations at Lincoln's Inn Fields Theatre. To retrieve the credit of his theatre Rich created a species of dramatic composition unknown to this, and, I believe, to any other country, which he called Pantomime. It consisted of two parts, one serious, the other comic; by the help of gay scenes, fine habits, grand dances, appropriate music, and other decorations, he exhibited a story from "Ovid's Metamorphosis," or some other fabulous history. Between the pauses of the acts he interwove a comic fable, consisting chiefly of the courtship of Harlequin and Columbine, with a variety of surprising adventures and tricks, which were produced by the magic wand of Harlequin; such as the sudden transformation of palaces and temples to huts and cottages; of men and women into wheelbarrows and joint stools; of trees turned to houses; colonnades to beds of tulips; and mechanics' hops into serpents and ostriches.

It is a most remarkable fact that the Pantomimes that Rich brought out, all of them could be written down as successes. In the exhibition of his Pantomimes, Mr. Rich always displayed the greatest taste. He had also acquired a considerable reputation as a performer of the motley hero under the name of "Lun Junr," as he was so designated on the bills at that time, and he was the first performer who rendered the character of Harlequin at all intelligible in this country. To others he taught the art of silent, but expressive, action, the interpreter of the mind. Feeling was pre-eminent in his Miming; and he used to render the scene of a separation with Columbine as graphic as it was affecting. Excellent were his "statue scenes" and his "catching the butterfly;" so also were his other dumb show performances.

Of Rich, Garrick wrote:—

"When Lun appeared with matchless art and whim,

He gave the power of speech to every limb;

Though masked and mute conveyed his quick intent,

And told in frolic's gestures all he meant."

Rich, however, erred in thinking himself a better actor than a Pantomimist; and, in fact, he thought himself a finer actor than the great Garrick himself. "You should see *me* play Richard!" was a favourite cry of his.

In 1782, after seeing the Pantomime of "Robinson Crusoe," Walpole said, "How unlike the Pantomimes of Rich, which were full of wit, and coherent, and carried on by a story."

As I have shown above, Rich had, like many other people, his own particular little idiosyncrasies, and when in the season 1746-7 he netted nearly £9,000 from his Pantomimes, to the chagrin of Garrick and Quin, he was very angry and much annoyed because he, as Harlequin, had contributed little or nothing. Another mannerism of his was to despise the regular drama on these occasions, and he has been known to look at the packed audience through a small hole in the curtain, and then ejaculate, "Ah! you are there, you fools, are you? Much good may it do you!"

Rich used to address everyone as "Mister." On one occasion Foote, being incensed at being so addressed, asked Rich why he did not call him by his name. "Don't be angry," says Rich, "I sometimes forget my own name." "I know," replied Foote, "that you can't write your own name, but I wonder you should forget it."

The first of Rich's successes was "Harlequin Sorcerer." On its production Pope wrote:—

"Behold a sober sorcerer rise

Swift to whose wand a winged volume flies;

All sudden, gorgon's hiss and dragon's glare,

And ten horned fiends and giants rush to war.

Hell rises, heaven descends, and dance on earth,

Gods, imps and monsters, music, rage and mirth,

A fire, a jig, a battle, and a ball,

Till one wide conflagration swallows all;

Thence a new world to nature's laws unknown,

Breaks out refulgent with a heaven its own;

Another Cynthia her new journey runs,

And other planets circle after suns.

The forests dance, the rivers upwards rise,

Whales sport in woods, and dolphins in the skies;

At last, to give the whole creation grace,

Lo! one vast egg produces human race."

Of Harlequin, in "Harlequin Sorcerer," being hatched from an egg by the rays of the sun. This has been called a master-piece of Rich's Miming "From the first chipping of the egg (says Jackson) his receiving of motion, his feeling of the ground, his standing upright, to his quick Harlequin trip round the empty shell, through the whole progression, every limb had its tongue, and every motion a voice."

As probably occurring in "Harlequin Sorcerer," there is an amusing incident. The belief in the possibility of a supernatural appearance on the stage existed (says an old writer) about the beginning of the eighteenth century. A dance of infernals having to be exhibited, they were represented in dresses of black and red, with fiery eyes and snaky locks, and garnished with every pendage of horror. They were twelve in number. In the middle of their performance, while intent upon the figure in which they had been completely practised, an actor of some humour, who had been accommodated with a spare dress, appeared among them. He was, if possible, more terrific than the rest, and seemed to the beholders as designed by the conductor for the principal fiend. His fellow furies took the alarm; they knew he did not belong to them, and they judged him an infernal in earnest. Their fears were excited, a general panic ensued, and the whole group fled different ways; some to their dressing-rooms, and others, through the streets, to their own homes, in order to avoid the destruction which they believed to be coming upon them, for the profane mockery they had been guilty of. The odd devil was *non inventus*. He took himself invisibly away, through fears of another kind. He was, however, seen by many, in imagination, to fly through the roof of the house, and they fancied themselves almost suffocated by the stench he had left behind. The confusion of the audience is scarcely to be described. They retired to their families, informing them of this supposed appearance of the devil, with many of his additional frolics in the exploit. So thoroughly was its reality believed that every official assurance which could be made the following day did not entirely counteract the idea. The explanation was given by Rich himself, in the presence of his friend Bencraft, the contriver, and perhaps the actor of the scheme, which he designed only as an innocent affair, to confuse the dancers, without adverting to the serious consequences which succeeded.

I have met with another author, who, in giving an account of this transaction, places it as a much earlier period, and says it was during the performance of "Dr. Faustus," and that when the devil took flight he carried away with him the roof of the theatre. This story may be alluded to in a very curious work, entitled, "The Blacke Booke" (a proper depository), "London, printed in black letter, by T.C. for Jeffery Chorlton, 1604." "The light burning serjant Lucifer" says of one, running away through fear of fire at a brothel, "Hee had a head of hayre like one of my divells in 'Doctor Faustus,' when the olde theatre crakt and frighted the audience."

Emulating Rich, Drury Lane then followed with "Mars and Venus," of which Colley Cibber says: Was formed into something more than motion without meaning into a connected presentation of dances in character, wherein the passions were so happily expressed, and the whole story so intelligibly told by a mute narration of gesture only, that even thinking spectators allowed it to be both a pleasing and a rational entertainment; though, at the same time, from our distrust of its reception we durst not venture to decorate it with any extraordinary expense of scenes or habits; but upon the success of this attempt it was rightly concluded that if a visible expense in both were added to something of the same nature, it could not fail of drawing the town proportionately after it.

From this original hint there (but every way unequal to it) sprang forth that succession of monstrous medlies, that have so long infested the stage, and which arose upon one another alternately, at both houses, outvying in expense, like contending bribes on both sides at an election, to secure a majority of the multitude.

If I am asked (after condemning these fooleries myself) how I came to assent or continue my share of expense to them? I have no better excuse for my error, than confessing it. I did it against my conscience, and had not virtue enough to starve by opposing a multitude that would have been too hard for me.

("The Drama's laws the Drama's patrons give," has always been an axiom of the stage; and worthy Colley Cibber, notwithstanding his antagonism, and the rivalry of Rich, had too good a knowledge of this truism not to do otherwise but follow the popular voice.)

Notwithstanding then (Cibber continues) this, our compliance with the vulgar taste, we generally made use of these Pantomimes, but as crutches to our weakest plays. Nor were we so lost to all sense of what was valuable, as to dishonor our best authors in such bad company. We still had a due respect to several select plays, that were able to be their own support; and in which we found constant account, without painting and patching them out.... It is a reproach to a sensible people to let folly so quickly govern their pleasures.

Henry Fielding, the novelist, was one of Harlequin's assailants. "The comic part of the English Pantomimes," he says, "being duller than anything before shown on the stage could only be set off by the superlative dulness of the serious portion, in which the gods and goddesses were so insufferably tedious, that Harlequin was always a relief from still worse company." Eager for theatrical reform, the "Weekly Miscellany" of 1732, said that plays were not intended for tradesmen, and denounced Pantomimes as infamous.

Another competitor, who entered the lists against Rich, was Thormond, a dancing-master, and at Drury Lane Theatre he produced "Dr. Faustus," in 1733. Speaking of this Pantomime, Pasquin mentions that "An account is very honestly published, to save people the trouble of going to see it."

In a Pantomime produced at Drury Lane in the following year, there were Macklin, Theo. Cibber (who ultimately lost his life by shipwreck in the Irish Sea, in company with a troupe of Pantomimists), Mrs. Clive, and Mrs. Cibber. At the performance it was announced that the money paid would be returned to anyone who went out before the overture; but no one availed themselves of the concession. Commenting on the occurrence, a contemporary writer observes:— "Happy is it that we live in an age of taste, when the dumb eloquence and natural wit and humour of Harlequin are justly preferred to the whining of Tragedy, or the vulgarity of Comedy."

Garrick, at Drury Lane, finding his audience with no heart for tragedy, and that they must have Pantomime, very wisely said, "If you won't come to 'Lear' and 'Hamlet,' I must give you Harlequin." And Harlequin he did give them, in the person of Woodward, one of the best of Harlequins that ever trod the stage. A contemporary print of the time, represents Woodward being weighed in one scale, with all the great actors of the day in the other, and Woodward makes them all kick the beam.

To satirise the prevailing fashion, Garrick penned the following:—

They in the drama find no joys,

But doat on mimicry and toys;

Thus, when a dance is on my bill,

Nobility my boxes fill;

Or send three days before the time

To crowd a new-made Pantomime.

Garrick's success, however, was, I am of opinion, undoubtedly owing to his being such a clever Pantomimist. "We saw him," says Grimm, "play the dagger scene in 'Macbeth' in a room in his ordinary dress, without any stage illusion; and, as he followed with his eyes the air-drawn dagger, he became so grand that the assembly broke into a cry of general admiration. Who would believe that this same man, a moment after, counterfeited, with equal perfection, a pastry cook's boy, who, carrying a tray of tartlets on his head, and gaping about him at the corner of the street, lets his tray fall, and, at first stupified by the accident, bursts at last into a fit of crying?"

All our great actors have been good Mimics, and herein, doubtless, lies the secret of their success. The mere intonation of words unaccompanied by a strict knowledge of "that dumb, silent language," Pantomime, is only *parroting*. Herein, therefore, lies the true imitativeness of the actor, and *the natural form of acting*. The word actor "Is a name only given to the persons in a dramatic work, *because they ought to be in continual action during the performance of it*." It does not mean that the actor is to stand still, and to be in action only with his tongue when speaking his "lines." No! he bears the honoured name of actor, and he should bring the full power of gesture language—Pantomime—that he has at his control into play in order to be convincing in the character that, for the time being, he is.

Action (mentions Betterton, in his "History of the English Stage," 1741), can never be in its perfection but on the stage. Action, indeed, has a natural excellence in it superior to all other qualities; action is motion, and motion is the support of nature, which without it would sink into the sluggish mass of chaos. Life is motion, and when that ceases, the human body so beautiful, nay so divine, when enlivened by motion, becomes a dead and putrid corpse, from which all turn their eyes. The eye is caught by anything in motion, but passes over the sluggish and motionless things as not the pleasing object of its view.

The natural power of motion, or action, is the reason that the attention of the audience is fixed by any irregular, or even fantastic action, on the stage, of the most indifferent player; and supine and drowsy when the best actor speaks without the addition of action. The stage ought to be the seat of passion in its various kinds, and, therefore, the actors ought to be thoroughly acquainted with the whole nature of the affections, and habits of the mind, or else they will never be able to express them justly in their looks and gestures, as well as in the tone of their voice and manner of utterance. They must know them in their various mixtures, as they are differently blended together in the different characters they represent; and then that excellent rule in the "Essay on Poetry" will be of equal use to the poet and player:—

Who must look within to find

These *secret* turns of Nature in the mind;

Without this part in vain would be the whole,

And but a *body* all without a soul?

A few words more just to lay further stress on the importance of Pantomime, and then to return to our History. Take any part in any play, strip from it in its enactment the whole of its gesture language, could we realise that the actor appearing in it was portraying nature for us? Replace the Pantomime so essential to the part, and the character becomes—or rather should become if properly played—a creature of flesh and blood the same as ourselves. Pantomime, on the other hand, does not require words to be spoken to express its meaning, as it is quite expressible without.

A contemporary account of the production of the Pantomime "Harlequin Dr. Faustus," at Drury Lane Theatre, forms interesting reading, in addition to providing a contrast with present-day Pantomime.

Every action is executed to different agreeable music, so adapted that it properly expresses what is going forward; in the machinery there is something so highly surprising that words cannot give a full idea of it. The effects described seem to be marvellous, considering the state of theatrical mechanism. A devil riding on a fiery dragon rides swiftly across the stage. Two country men and women enter to be told their fortunes, when Dr. Faustus waves his wand, and four pictures turn out of the scenes opposite, representing a judge and a soldier, a dressed lady, and a lady in riding habit; the scene changes to the outside of a handsome house, when the louting men, running in, place their backs against the door. The front of the house turns, and at the same instant the machine turns, a supper ready dressed rises up. The countrymen's wives remain with the Doctor, who (afterwards) goes out. He beckons the table, and it follows him. Punch, Scaramouch, and Pierrot are next met by the Doctor, who invites them into a banquet. The table ascends into the air. He waves his wand, and asses' ears appear at the sides of their heads. A usurer lending money to Dr. Faustus demands a limb as security, and cuts off the Doctor's leg, several legs appear on the scene, and the Doctor strikes a woman's leg with his wand, which immediately flies from the rest, and fixes to the Doctor's stump, who dances with it ridiculously. The next scene opens, disclosing the Doctor's study. He enters affrighted, and the clock strikes one; the figures of Time and Death appear. Several devils enter and tear him in pieces, some sink, some fly out, each bearing a limb of him. The last, which is the grand scene, is the most magnificent that ever appeared on the English stage—all the gods and goddesses discovered with the apotheosis of Diana, ascending into the air.

The tricks that formed part and parcel of the Pantomimes, in causing surprise and wonderment, placed Harlequin, for his extraordinary feats, in the first rank of magicians. Oftentimes, however, they were the cause of many accidents.

Chetwood—William Rufus Chetwood—who had, in the eighteenth century, a bookseller's shop in Covent Garden, and was, for twenty years, prompter for Drury Lane, a writer of four plays, and a volume of sketches of the actors whom he had met, says:—"A tumbler at the Haymarket beat the breath out of his body by an accident, and which raised such vociferous applause that lasted the poor man's life, for he never breathed more. Indeed, his wife had this comfort, when the truth was known, pity succeeded to the roar of applause. Another accident occurred in the Pantomime of 'Dr. Faustus' (previously referred to), at Lincoln's Inn Fields Theatre, where a machine in the working threw the mock Pierrot down headlong with such force that the poor man broke a plank on the stage with his fall, and expired; another was sorely maimed that he did not survive many days; and a third, one of the softer sex, broke her thigh."

Vandermere, the Harlequin, one of the most agile that ever trod the stage, on one occasion, in the pursuit by the Clown, leaped through a window on to the stage, a full thirteen feet. Performing at the Dublin theatre one night, having a prodigious leap to make, the persons behind the scenes not being ready to receive him in the customary blanket, he fell upon the stage and was badly bruised. This accident occasioned him to take a solemn oath that he would never take another leap upon the stage; nor did he violate his oath, for when he afterwards played Harlequin another actor of his size, and of considerable activity was equipped with the parti-coloured habit, and when a leap was necessary Vandermere passed off on one side of the stage as Dawson—Vandermere's understudy—entered at the other, and undertook it.

How little do we know of the tragic ending of these poor unhappy Pantomimists' lives. Their names even have not been handed down to us, and they, like probably many more with whose quips and quiddities we have laughed at with infinite zest, have long since gone "to that bourne from whence no traveller returns," and perhaps, "unwept, unhonoured, and unsung."

On February 12, 1739, Rich produced, at Covent Garden (opened in December 1732, with Congreve's "Way of the World"), "Orpheus and Eurydice." On the mounting something like £2,000 were spent.

Rich devised the scenario and comic scenes. Lewis Theobald wrote the libretto, and George Lambert—founder of the Beefsteak Club—painted the scenery. Hippisley played Clown, Manager Rich was the Harlequin, and Signor Grimaldi, father of the celebrated Mime, to be noted further on, was the Pantaloon. This is the first instance of a member of the Grimaldi family (says Mr. W.J. Lawrence) appearing in English Pantomime.

The following was the argument and the curious arrangement of the scenes:—Interlude I.—Rhodope, Queen of Thrace, practising art magic, makes love to Orpheus. He rejects her love. She is enraged. A serpent appears who receives Rhodope's commands, and these ended, glides off the stage. Here the comic part begins. In the Opera (as practically it was) a scene takes place between Orpheus and Eurydice. Eurydice's heel is pierced by the serpent, behind the scenes. She dies on the stage—after which the comic part is continued. Interlude II. Scene: Hell. Pluto and Orpheus enter. Orpheus prevails on Pluto to restore Eurydice to him. Ascalox tells Orpheus that Eurydice shall follow him, but that if he should look back at her before they shall have passed the bounds of Hell, she will die again. Orpheus turns back to look for Eurydice, Fiends carry her away. After this the comic part is resumed. Interlude III.— Orpheus again rejects Rhodope's solicitations. Departs. The scene draws, and discovers Orpheus slain. Several Baccants enter in a triumphant manner. They bring in the lyre and chaplet of Orpheus. Rhodope stabs herself. The piece concludes with the remainder of the comic part.

"'The Scots Magazine' for March, 1740, says:—'Orpheus and Eurydice' draws the whole town to Covent Garden, whether for the Opera itself (the words of which are miserable stuff) or for the Pantomimical Interlude, with which it is intermixed, I cannot determine. The music is pretty good, and the tricks are not foolisher than usual, and some have said that they have more meaning than most that have preceded them. The performance is grand as to the scenery. What pleases everybody is a regular growth of trees, represented more like nature than what has yet been seen upon the stage, and the representation of a serpent so lively as to frighten half the ladies who see it. It is, indeed, curious in its kind, being wholly a piece of machinery, that enters, performs its exercise of head, body, and tail in a most surprising manner, and makes behind the curtain with a velocity scarcely credible. It is about a foot and a half in circumference of the thickest part, and far exceeds the former custom of stuffing a bag into such likeness. It is believed to have cost more than £200; and when the multitude of wings, springs, etc., whereof it consists, are considered, the charge will not appear extravagant. The whole Royal family have been to see this performance; and, from what can be judged, everybody else will see it before the end of the season, the house being every day full at 3 o'clock, though seldom empty till after eleven."

Sam Hoole—father of the translator of Tasso and Ariosto— was Rich's chief machinist at this period, and the inventor of this famous serpent. He had, according to Cumberland, a shop where he sold mechanical toys. Having a large stock of serpent toys left on his hands he became a ruined and bankrupt man.

"Orpheus and Eurydice" was revived by Rich in 1747, and again in 1755; when it ran 31 nights. In 1768 it was reproduced by his successors at Covent Garden. In October, 1787, it was again put in the bill, and this time by Royal Command, it was said.

Of the number of Pantomimes brought out by Rich I shall not dilate on, and those that I have referred to will, doubtless, show what all these "plays without words" were like.

During the summer season of 1761, at Drury Lane, Murphy and Foote endeavoured

"From Pantomime to free the stage

And combat all the ministers of the age,"

by ridiculing the popular amusement in having the character of Harlequin hung in full view of the audience in a play entitled "The Wishes." When the catastrophe was at hand Murphy whispered to Cumberland: "If they don't damn this, they deserve to be damned themselves!" No sooner were the words uttered than a turbulent mob in the pit broke out, and quickly put an end to the dire fatality with which Pantomime and its hero, Harlequin, were threatened.

Christopher Rich gave the first engagement to the afterwards celebrated actress, Mrs. Oldfield, and, previously, a similar kindness to Robert Wilks, about the year 1690, at the salary of fifteen shillings a week, with two shillings and sixpence deducted for teaching him to dance. Another famous performer, Macklin, was also introduced to the stage by this family.

At the Lincoln's Inn Fields Theatre, in 1721, there was a memorable riot, caused by some drunken aristocratic beaux, owing to an alleged insult, which one of their number was supposed to have received. The beau referred to, a noble Earl, had crossed the stage whilst Macbeth and his lady were upon it, in order to speak to a companion who was lolling in the wings. Rich told the noble Earl that for his indecorum he would not be allowed behind the scenes again, which so incensed the latter that he gave Manager Rich a smart slap on the face, which Rich returned. Swords then were drawn, and between the actors and the beaux a free fight ensued, which ended in the former driving the latter out of the theatre. The rioters, however, again obtained access, and rushing into the boxes, cut down the hangings, besides doing other damage, when, led by Quin and a number of constables, several of the beaux were captured, and taken before the magistrates. The end of it all was that the matter was compromised; but, in order to prevent a recurrence of such disorderly scenes, a guard should attend the performances. The custom of having the military in attendance at our theatres—which the above affray was the primary cause—was in vogue for over a hundred years after this event.

Rich lived to see Pantomimes firmly established at Drury Lane and Covent Garden. Drury Lane did, for a few years, discard it in favour of spectacle, but ultimately found it advisable to return to Pantomime.

At the beginning of the 'sixties of the eighteenth century—1761—died the father of Harlequins in England, and also—as he has been called—of English Pantomimes, and there is, I believe, a costly tomb erected to his memory in Hillingdon Church-yard, Middlesex.

Rich left Covent Garden Theatre to his son-in-law, Beard, the vocalist, with the not unpleasant restriction, however, that the property should be sold when £60,000 was bid for it, and for which sum it ultimately passed into the hands of Harris, Colman, and their partners.

CHAPTER XVI. JOSEPH GRIMALDI.

The year 1778 marks an epoch in the History of Pantomime, as just over three-quarters of a century before marked another epoch, the introduction of Pantomimes to the English stage. On December 18th, 1778, was born Joseph Grimaldi—afterwards the Prince of Clowns, and the son of Giuseppe Grimaldi ("Iron Legs"). Joe's first appearance was at Sadler's Wells on April 16, Easter Monday, 1781, he not being quite three years old. Dickens, in the "Memoirs of Grimaldi," has given us from the Clown's own diary, which Grimaldi kept close up to the time of his death, on May, 31st, 1837, a full and true account of the life of this remarkably clever Pantomimist. To add to what Dickens has written of "Only a Clown" (which doubtless the reader is already acquainted with) would only be like painting the lily; and, perhaps, I cannot do better in honouring his memory than by quoting the words of Mr. Harley at the annual dinner of the Drury Lane Fund, spoken in the June following Grimaldi's death:—"Yet, shall delicacy suffer no violence in adducing one example, for death has hushed his cock-crowing cachination, and uproarious merriment. The mortal Jupiter of practical Joke, the Michael Angelo of buffoonery, who, if he was *Grim-all-day*, was sure to make you chuckle at night."

A contemporary writer of Grimaldi's days thus eulogises the Prince of Clowns:—

As a Clown, Mr. Grimaldi is perfectly unrivalled. Other performers of the part may be droll in their generation; but, which of them can for a moment compete with the Covent Garden hero in acute observation upon the foibles and absurdities of society, and his happy talent of holding them up to ridicule. He is the finest practical satyrist that ever existed. He does not, like many Clowns, content himself with raising a horse-laugh by contortions and grimaces, but tickles the fancy, and excites the risibility of an audience by devices as varied as they are ingenious. "He uses his folly as a stalking-horse, under cover of which he shoots his wit;" and fully deserves the encomium bestowed upon him by Kemble, who, it is said, pronounced him to be "the best low comedian upon the stage."

There are few things, we think, more delightful than a Pantomime—that is, a *good* Pantomime, such as is usually produced at Covent Garden. We know there are a set of solemn pompous mortals about town, who express much dignified horror at the absurdities of these things, and declaim very fluently, in good set terms, upon the necessity of their abolition. Such fellows as these are ever your dullest of blockheads. Conscious of their lack of ideas, they think to earn the reputation of men of sterling sense, by inveighing continually against what *they* deem to be frivolity; while they only expose more clearly to all observers the sad vacuum which exists in their *pericraniums*. Far, far from us be such dullards, and such opinions; and let us continue to laugh heartily at our Pantomimes, undisturbed by their tedious harangues; "Do they think, because they are *wise*, there shall be no more cakes and ale?" The man who refuses to smile at the humours of Grimaldi is made of bad materials— *hic niger est*—let no such man be trusted!

Can there possibly be a more captivating sight than that which the theatre presents nightly, of hundreds of beautiful children all happy and laughing, "as if a master-spring constrained them all;" and filled with delight, unalloyed and unbounded, at the performance of one man? And shall that man go without his due meed of praise? Never be it said! No, Joey! When we forget thee, may our right hand forget its cunning! We owe thee much for the delight thou hast already afforded us; and rely upon thee, with confident expectation, for many a future hour of gay forgetfulness. Well do we remember, in our boyish dreams of bliss, how prominent a feature thou didst stand amongst the anticipated enjoyments of Christmas; how the thoughts of home, of kindred, and release from school, were rendered ten-fold more delightful by the idea of thy motley garb and mirth-inspiring voice, which ever formed the greatest enjoyment our holidays afforded. Heaven be praised, we still are children in some respects, for we still feel gladdened by thy gambols, as heartily as we did years ago, when we made our periodical escape from the terrors of our old pedagogue's frown, and went with Aunt Bridget ("Happier than ourselves the while") to banquet upon the Pantomimic treat provided for us. "All wisdom is folly," says the philosopher; but we often incline to think the converse of the proposition correct, when we see thee put thy antic disposition on, and set the audience in a roar by the magic of thy powers.

It is thought by many persons that Grimaldi is seen to greater advantage on the small stage of Sadler's Wells, than on the more capacious one of Covent Garden; but, this is an opinion with which we cannot coincide. He always appears to us more at his ease at the latter house; to come forth exulting in his power, and exclaiming, "Ay, marry, here my soul hath elbow-room." His engagement there has certainly been a lucrative speculation for the proprietors. "Mother Goose," we believe, drew more money than any other piece which has been produced during the present century; and no Pantomime since brought forward at Covent Garden has been unsuccessful; which is mainly to be attributed to his inimitable performance of Clown. It is scarcely possible for language to do justice to his unequalled powers of gesture and expression. Do our readers recollect a Pantomime some years ago, in which he was introduced begging a tart from a pieman? The simple expression, "May I?" with the look and action which accompanied it, are impressed upon our recollection, as forming one of the finest pieces of acting we ever witnessed. Indeed, let the subject be what it may, it never fails to become highly amusing in the hands of Grimaldi; whether it is to rob a pieman, or open an oyster, imitate a chimney-sweep, or a dandy, grasp a red-hot poker, or devour a pudding, take snuff, sneeze, make love, mimic a tragedian, cheat his master, pick a pocket, beat a watchman, or nurse a child, it is all performed in so admirably humorous and extravagantly natural a manner, that spectators of the most saturnine disposition are irresistibly moved to laughter.

Mr. Grimaldi also possesses great merit in Pantomimic performances of a different character, which all are aware of, who have ever seen him in the melodrama, called "Perouse," and other pieces of the same description.

We cannot better terminate this article, than with a poetical tribute to his powers, addressed to him by one of the authors of "Horace in London," who appears to have had a true relish of his subject:—

Facetious Mime! thou enemy of gloom,

Grandson of Momus, blithe and debonair,

Who, aping Pan, with an inverted broom,

Can'st brush the cobwebs from the brows of care.

Our gallery gods immortalize thy song;

Thy Newgate thefts impart ecstatic pleasure;

Thou bid'st a Jew's harp charm a Christian throng,

A Gothic salt-box teem with attic treasure.

When Harlequin, entangled in thy clue,

By magic seeks to dissipate the strife,

Thy furtive fingers snatch his faulchion too;

The luckless wizard loses wand and wife.

The fabled egg from thee obtains its gold;

Thou sett'st the mind from critic bondage loose,

Where male and female cacklers, young and old,

Birds of a feather, hail the sacred Goose.

Even pious souls, from Bunyan's durance free,

At Sadler's Wells applaud thy agile wit,

Forget old Care while they remember thee,

"Laugh the heart's laugh," and haunt the jovial pit.

Long may'st thou guard the prize thy humour won,

Long hold thy court in Pantomimic state,

And, to the equipoise of English fun,

Exalt the lowly, and bring down the great.

Again we are told "That his Pantomime was such that you could fancy he would have been the Pulcinello of the Italians, the Harlequin of the French, that he could have returned a smart repartee from Carlin. His motions, eccentric as they were, were evidently not a mere lesson from the gymnasium; there was a will and mind overflowing with, nay living upon fun, real fun. He was so extravagantly natural, that the most saturnine looker-on acknowledged his sway; and neither the wise, the proud, or the fair, the young nor the old, were ashamed to laugh till tears coursed down their cheeks at Joe and his comicalities."

Grimaldi used sometimes to play in two different Pantomimes at two different theatres, when he would have to go through some twenty scenes.

Unlike the painting of the face with a few patches adopted by the modern Clown, Grimaldi used to give one the idea of a greedy boy, who had covered himself with jam in robbing from a cupboard. Grimaldi dressed the part like a Clown should be dressed. His trousers were large and baggy, and were fastened to his jacket, and round his neck he wore a schoolboy's frill—part of the dress, in all probability, borrowed from the Spanish Captain and the French Pierrot.

At Drury Lane on Friday, June 27, 1828, he took his farewell benefit. The following being the bill:—

Mr. Grimaldi's Farewell Benefit, On Friday, June 27th, 1828, will be performed JONATHAN IN ENGLAND, after which A MUSICAL MELANGE, To be succeeded by THE ADOPTED CHILD, and concluded by HARLEQUIN HOAX, In which Mr. Grimaldi will act Clown in one scene, sing a song, and speak his FAREWELL ADDRESS.

With the reader's permisson, I will give, from his "Memoirs," the address he spoke:—

"Ladies and Gentlemen:—In putting off the Clown's garment, allow me to drop also the Clown's taciturnity, and address you in a few parting sentences. I entered early on this course of life, and leave it prematurely. Eight-and-forty years only have passed over my head—but I am going as fast down the hill of life as that older Joe—John Anderson. Like vaulting ambition, I have overleaped myself, and pay the penalty in an advanced old age. If I have now any aptitude for tumbling it is through bodily infirmity, for I am worse on my feet than I used to be on my head. It is four years since I jumped my last jump—filched my last oyster—boiled my last sausage—and set in for retirement. Not quite so well provided for, I must acknowledge, as in the days of my Clownship, for then, I dare say, some of you remember, I used to have a fowl in one pocket and sauce for it in the other.

"To-night has seen me assume the motley for a short time—it clung to my skin as I took it off, and the old cap and bells rang mournfully as I quitted them for ever.

"With the same respectful feelings as ever do I find myself in your presence—in the presence of my last audience—this kindly assemblage so happily contradicting the adage that a favourite has no friends. For the benvolence that brought you hither—accept, ladies and gentlemen, my warmest and most grateful thanks, and believe, that of one and all, Joseph Grimaldi takes a double leave, with a farewell on his lips, and a tear in his eyes.

"Farewell! That you and yours may ever enjoy that greatest earthly good—health, is the sincere wish of your faithful and obliged servant. God bless you all!"

Poor Joe was buried in the burying-ground of St. James' Chapel, on Pentonville Hill, and in a grave next to his friend, Charles Dibdin. May the earth lie lightly over him!

CHAPTER XVII. PLOTS OF THE OLD FORM OF PANTOMIMES

—A DESCRIPTION OF "HARLEQUIN AND THE OGRESS; OR THE SLEEPING BEAUTY OF THE WOOD," PRODUCED AT COVENT GARDEN—GRIMALDI, *PÈRE ET FILS*—TOM ELLAR, THE HARLEQUIN, AND BARNES, THE PANTALOON—AN ACCOUNT OF THE FIRST PRODUCTION OF THE "HOUSE THAT JACK BUILT," AT COVENT GARDEN—SPECTACULAR DISPLAY—ANTIQUITY AND ORIGIN OF SOME PANTOMIMIC DEVICES—DEVOTO, ANGELO, AND FRENCH, THE SCENIC ARTISTS—TRANSPARENCIES—BEVERLEY— TRANSFORMATION SCENES.

Of the plots of the old form of Pantomime and what these entertainments were generally like, graphically, does Planché describe them.

How different (he says) were the Christmas Pantomimes of my younger days. A pretty story—a nursery tale— dramatically told, in which "the course of true love never did run smooth," formed the opening; the characters being a cross-grained old father, with a pretty daughter, who had two suitors—one a poor young fellow, whom she preferred, the other a wealthy fop, whose pretensions were, of course, favoured by the father. There was also a body servant of some sort in the old man's establishment. At the moment when the young lady was about to be forcibly married to the fop she despised, or, on the point of eloping with the youth of her choice, the good fairy made her appearance, and, changing the refractory pair into Harlequin and Columbine, the old curmudgeon into Pantaloon, and the body servant into Clown: the two latter in company with the rejected "lover," as he was called, commenced the pursuit of the happy pair, and the "comic business" consisted of a dozen or more cleverly constructed scenes, in which all the tricks and changes had a meaning, and were introduced as contrivances to favour the escape of Harlequin and Columbine, when too closely followed by their enemies.

There was as regular a plot as might be found in a melodrama. An interest in the chase which increased the admiration of the ingenuity and the enjoyment of the fun of the tricks, by which the runaways escaped capture, till the inevitable "dark scene" came, a cavern or a forest, in which they were overtaken, seized, and the magic wand, which had so uniformly aided them, snatched from the grasp of the despairing Harlequin, and flourished in triumph by the Clown. Again at the critical moment the protecting fairy appeared, and, exacting the consent of the father to the marriage of the devoted couple, transported the whole party to what was really a grand last scene, which everybody did wait for. There was some congruity, some dramatic construction, in such Pantomimes; and then the acting. For it was acting, and first-rate acting.

To give the reader a further insight into the old form of Christmas Pantomimes, I cull the following from "The Drama," a contemporary magazine of the period (1822):—

In compliance with the long-established custom of gratifying the holiday visitors of the theatres with Pantomimic representations at this season of year, a new piece of that description was produced at this theatre (Covent Garden) last night, December 26th, 1822, under the title of "Harlequin and the Ogress; or the Sleeping Beauty of the Wood." The introductory story is taken from the well-known tale of "The Sleeping Beauty," in "Mother Bunch's Fairy Tales," which had before been "melodramatised," but had not hitherto been taken for the groundwork of a Harlequinade.

The piece opens in one of the fabled grand caverns under the Pyramids of Egypt, in which the three fatal sisters of Mother Bunch's Mythology are seen spinning and winding a ball of golden thread, the fastening of which to the wrist of the Sleeping Beauty is intended to add another century to the duration of her life, and of the power which the Ogress, or Fairy, has exercised over her, and her possessions, for the preceding hundred years. The ball having been completed, with the due quantum of magic incantation in such cases prescribed, is consigned to the care of Grim Gribber, the porter of the castle, with directions to attach it to the wrist of the lady in the chamber of sleep, whither he accordingly proceeds for that purpose; but overcome by the soporific influences of the atmosphere of that enchanted place, he falls into a deep sleep ere his task is accomplished. The Prince Azoff, with his Squire Abnab, straying from a hunting party into the enchanted cedar grove, encounters the Fairy Blue-bell, protector of the Sleeping Beauty, who imparts to the Prince the story of her enchantment, furnishes him with a magic flower to protect him from the influence of the Ogress, and instructs him in the means of releasing the Beauty at the expiration of the term of her first enchanted sleep, which is then drawing to a close. In the amazement which seizes the Prince on finding himself in the chamber of sleep, at the splendour of everything around him, and the sight of the Sleeping Beauty with her surrounding train of attendants, whose faculties are all enchained in the same preternatural slumber, he lets fall the magic flower, and becomes thereby subject to the power of the Ogress, from which he is, however, rescued on the instant by the protecting interference of the Fairy Blue-bell. But in punishment of his neglect, he is condemned to wander for a time in search of happiness with the now-awakened Beauty, pursued by the relentless Ogress and her servant, Grim Gribber. The whole of the persons engaged in the scene now undergo the prescriptive Pantomimic changes, and the ordinary succession of Harlequinade adventures, tricks, and transformations ensue.

Our old favourites, the Grimaldis, father and son, Mr. Ellar as Harlequin, and Mr. Barnes as Pantaloon, were hailed, on their appearance, with the warmth of greeting to which their excellence in their several parts fully entitles them, and displayed their wonted drollery, gracefulness, and agility: and Miss Brissak, who, for the first time, appeared as Columbine, acquitted herself with tolerable credit, and was very well received.

The scenery in general was marked with that characteristic beauty and highly-finished excellence, which have long distinguished the productions of this theatre: and the panoramic series of views of the River Thames, from Greenwich to the Nore, on the passage of the Royal flotilla for Scotland, and its arrival in Leith Roads, probably surpass everything of the kind before exhibited. There are several diverting tricks and ingenious changes. Grimaldi's equipment of a patent safety coach at Brighton, in particular was highly amusing. The machinery, which is, in many instances, of a most complicated description, worked remarkably well for a first night's exhibition; and the whole went off with a degree of *eclat*, which must have been exceedingly gratifying to the managers, as auguring the probability of such a lengthened run for the piece as may amply recompense the pains and expense which have been so lavishly bestowed in its preparation. The house was filled in every part, and the announcement of the Pantomime's repetition was received with the most clamorous approbation, undisturbed by a single dissentient voice.

The first production of "The House that Jack Built," at Covent Garden, on December 26, 1824, also reads interestingly:—

The Pantomime is before us, and we should ill-repay the pleasure it afforded us, if we did not acknowledge and make public its excellence. The name implies the source from which it is taken, and we had, therefore, the supreme pleasure of renewing our friendship with those very old acquaintances, the "Priest all shaven and shorn, the maiden all forlorn, the cow with the crumpled horn, the dog that worried the cat, that killed the rat, that eat up the malt, that lay in the House that Jack built." This, of course, gave us, as it appeared to do many others, great pleasure, "For should auld acquaintance be forgot, and never brought to mind." Mr. Farley, however, who supports (like an Atlas) all the weight of bringing forward these annual pieces of fun and foolery, and who appears to be as learned in the mystic lore of "hoary antiquity," as he is in the mysteries of all the wonders of the tricks, changes, and mechanism of the Pantomimic world, has let us this time into a secret, which will doubtless cause much erudite argument, and pros and cons from various sage antiquarians for months to come, in that invaluable work of old Sylvanus Urban, 'yclept the "Gentlemen's Magazine." As the play-bills on which this important piece of information is to be found, will doubtless be bought up by all the mystogogii of the Metropolis, and shortly become scarce, we shall take the liberty of inserting it in our imperishable pages, for the benefit, not only of posterity, but for those of our own day, who are infected with the building mania, and who, we think, ought to make Mr. Farley some very valuable present to mark their sense of the obligation they are under to him, in consequence of the benefit which must accrue to them from it. It appears from this fragment in what manner Jack became possessed of his house, and which it never before occurred to us, to enquire. Thus then the mystery is elucidated by Mr. Farley.

Jack's Wager;

"By virtue of one of our forest charters, if a man do build a dwelling upon common land, from sun-set to sun-rise, and enclose a piece of ground, wherein there shall be a tree growing, a beast feeding, a fire kindled, and provision in the pot, such dwelling shall be freely held by the builder, anything to the contrary, nevertheless, notwithstanding." Forest Laws.

Accordingly Jack, in the opening scene, is represented just before nightfall, as completing his dwelling, by putting on the chimney pot as the finishing stroke; he then claims his bride, Rosebud, from her father, Gaffer Gandy, who refuses his consent, having determined on bestowing her hand on one Squire Sap. Jack, in despair, repairs to Poor Robin, the village astrologer, who is intently observing an eclipse of the moon (which, by-the-bye, is most excellently managed), and relates his griefs. The old man cheers his drooping spirits, by casting his nativity and finding by his observations, that Jack's stars are of the most benign influence, and that all his wishes shall be fulfilled. The marriage of the maiden all forlorn with the Squire is on the point of being completed, when Venus (one of whose doves had been preserved by Jack) dispatches Cupid to the assistance of the despairing lovers, by the magic of whose powerful wand the usual Pantomimic changes are effected in a trice—Jack becomes Harlequin; Rosebud, Columbine; Gaffer, Pantaloon; the Squire, the Lover; and the Priest, the Clown. Mirth, revelry, fun, frolic, and joviality are now the order of the day, and the scene changes to a view of Hyde Park and the Serpentine River on a frosty morning in January: in which is represented, with admirable effect, a display of patent skating. An oil cloth is spread upon the stage, a group comprised of various laughable characters are assembled on it, and skate about with as much rapidity, and precisely as though it were a sheet of ice. The adroit skill of old stagers on the slippery surface, with the clumsy awkwardness and terror of novices in the art, are well represented. A prodigious fat man makes his appearance; when a race is called for, he, of course, tries his prowess, when the ice cracking beneath the heavy weight assembled on it gives way with a heavy crash, and "Fatty" is consigned to a watery bed. Assistance is immediately tendered, when, by Harlequin's power, a lean and shrivelled spirit of the deep rises from below to the great alarm of the beholders, and whose limbs continue to expand till his head touches the clouds. The whole of the scene is one of the most laughable and best managed in the Pantomime. Kew Gardens, on a May-day morning, is also a very pleasing scene, in which some pretty Morris dancing is introduced. The Barber's shop, in which shaving by steam is hit off, is excellent in its way, but not so well understood in its details, as to make it equally effective in representation. Vauxhall Bridge, and the Gardens which succeeds it, are also charmingly painted by the Grieves, and from hence the Clown and Pantaloon take an "Aeronautic excursion" to Paris. This is a revolving scene—the balloon ascends—and the English landscape gradually recedes from the view—the gradual approach of night—the rising of the moon—the passing of the balloon through heavy clouds—and the return of day, are beautifully represented; the sea covered with ships, is seen in distant perspective with the French coast; a bird's-eye view of Paris follows, and the balloon safely descends in the gardens of the Tuileries. The adjoining palace, mansions, and gardens being brilliantly illuminated, give the scene a most splendid and picturesque effect. A variety of other scenes, but far too numerous to mention individually, deserve the highest applause, particularly the village of Bow, Leadenhall Market, with a change to an illuminated civic feast in the Guildhall; Burlington Arcade at night, and the village of Ganderclue by sunrise. The Temple of Iris, formed of the "radiant panoply of the heavenly arch," by Grieve, is most brilliant.

The advent of Pantomime, early in the eighteenth century, gave a special fillip to spectacular display, as they were all announced to be set off with "new scenery, decorations, and flyings."

Some of the stage devices of Pantomime are of considerable antiquity; as, for instance, the basket-work hobby-horses, that figured as far back as the old English Morris dances, to be revived in the French ballet of the seventeenth century, and, in after years, in English Pantomime.

The Pantomime donkey is at least, we are told, 200 years old. In "*Arlequin Mercure Galant*," produced in Paris in 1682, by the Italian Comedians, Harlequin made his entrance on a moke's back—and the merriment afterwards being greatly enhanced when Master "Neddy," with Pan seated on its back, suddenly came in two, to the consternation of the beholders. To the Italian Pantomime Comedians we owe many of our stage devices and tricks. The statue scene in "Frivolity," played by the Messrs. Leopolds, was introduced by the Italians in "*Arlequin Lingere du Palais*," when this piece was performed at Paris in 1682. Again, the device of cutting a hole in a portrait for an eaves-dropper's head to be inserted, was used in "*Columbine Avocat*" as far back as 1685.

In "*Arlequin Lingere du Palais*," played at the Hotel de Bourgogne in October, 1682, there was represented two stalls—an underclothier's and a confectioner's. Harlequin dressed half like a man and half like a woman, with a mask on each side of his face to match presides in this dual capacity at both stalls. Pasquariel, who comes to buy, is utterly bewildered, and is made the target of both jests and missiles of monsieur of the confectioners, and mademoiselle of the adjoining stall. Possibly the shop scenes in our English Harlequinades may have originated from this. A similar idea to the above was given in O'Keefe's Pantomime of "Harlequin Teague; or the Giants' Causeway," performed at the Haymarket in 1782. Charles Bannister appeared in this Pantomime and sang a duet as a giant with two heads, one side representing a gentleman of quality, and the other a hunting squire. Mrs. German Reed, about 1855, appeared representing two old women, between whom an imaginary conversation was held, Mrs. Reed turning first one side of her face to the audience, and then the other. Fred Maccabe, in his "Essence of Faust," had also a similar allusion, and by many "transformation dancers" was it used. The antiquity of many other devices could be noted, but I must desist, yet I cannot help remarking that even here we have more exemplifications of history repeating itself.

Scenical representations and mechanical devices in Italy had long been made a fine art, and an English traveller and critic observes that our painting compared to theirs is only daubing. I find among their decorations statues of marble, alabaster, palaces, colonnades, galleries, and sketches of architecture; pieces of perspective that deceive the judgment as well as the eye; prospects of a prodigious extent in spaces not thirty feet deep. As for their machines I can't think it in the power of human wit to carry their inventions further. In 1697, I saw at Venice an elephant discovered on the stage, when, in an instant, an army was seen in its place; the soldiers, having by the disposition of their shields, given so true a representation of it as if it had been a real elephant.

In Rome, at the Theatre Capranio, in 1698, there was a ghost of a woman surrounded by guards. This phantom, extending her arms and unfolding her clothes, was, with one motion, transformed into a perfect palace, with its front, its wings, body, and courtyard. The guards, striking their halberds on the stage, were immediately turned into so many waterworks, cascades, and trees, that formed a charming garden before the palace. At the same theatre, in the opera "*Nerone Infante*," the interior of hell was shown. Here part of the stage opened, and discovered a scene underneath, representing several caves, full of infernal spirits, that flew about, discharging fire and smoke, on another side the river of Lethe and Charon's boat. Upon this landing a prodigious monster appeared, whose mouth opening to the great horror of the spectators, covered the front wings of the remaining part of the stage. Within his jaws was discovered a throne of fire, and a multitude of monstrous snakes, on which Pluto sat. After this the great monster, expanding his wings, began to move very slowly towards the audience. Under his body appeared a great multitude of devils, who formed themselves into a ballet, and plunged, one after the other, into the opening of the floor. The great monster was in an instant transformed into an innumerable multitude of broad white butterflies, which flew all into the pit, and so low that some often touched the hats of several of the spectators, and at last they disappeared. During this circumstance, which sufficiently employed the eyes of the spectators, the stage was refitted, and the scene changed into a beautiful garden, with which the third act began.

The scene painter, Devoto, painted the scenery and decorations for the Goodman's Fields Theatre, where, it is interesting to note, David Garrick made his first *London* appearance in 1741. His first appearance on any stage had been made at Ipswich on Tuesday, 21st July, in the same year, under the name of Lyddall. Garrick, during his time, introduced many novelties in the way of scenery and transparencies, acting on the suggestions of Signor Seivandoni, the scenic artist at the Opera-house, and the fencing master, Dominico Angelo. These transparencies became the talk of London, and it has been known for several plays to have been written so as to introduce them. The first transparent scene is said to have been the "Enchanted Wood," introduced in "Harlequin's Invasion," at Drury Lane, the painter being one French, the scenic artist of the theatre.

Beverley, the scene painter for Madame Vestris, half a century ago, brought fairy, or Pantomime, scenes to great perfection. Leopold Wagner, speaking of them, says:—"We have it upon the authority of Mr. Planché that these were almost entirely due to the skilled efforts and successes of Mr. William Beverley, who, in the nature of Extravaganza, so impressed the public with his fine talents as an artist upon theatrical canvas, that gorgeous scenes became quite the rage, and how, year after year, Mr. Beverley's powers were taxed to the utmost to outdo his former triumphs, and how the most costly materials and complicated machinery were annually put into requisition until the managers began to suffer."

Speaking of the production on the 26th December, 1849, of "The Island of Jewels," Planché says, "The novel, and yet exceedingly simple, falling of the leaves of a palm tree, which discovered six fairies, supporting a coronet of jewels, produced such an effect as I scarcely remember having witnessed on any similar occasion up to that period. The last scene became the first in the estimation of the management. The most complicated machinery, the most costly materials were annually put into requisition, until their bacon was so buttered that it was impossible to save it. Nothing was considered brilliant but the *last* scene. Dutch metal was in the ascendant. It was no longer even painting, it was upholstery. Mrs. Charles Mathews herself informed me that she had paid between £60 and £70 for gold tissue for the dresses of the Supernumeraries alone." I wonder what Mrs. Mathews would say if she could now visit this terrestrial sphere of ours?

All this love of spectacular display soon began to supersede the good old-fashioned Christmas Pantomimes.

In his work, "Behind the Scenes," Mr. Fitzgerald very graphically describes the Transformation scene of later days, and now becoming nearly as obsolete as the Harlequinade. All will recall in some elaborate transformation scene how quietly and gradually it is evoked. First the gauzes lift slowly one behind the other—perhaps the most pleasing of all scenic effects—giving glimpses of the Realms of Bliss seen beyond in a tantalising fashion. Then is revealed a kind of half glorified country, clouds and banks evidently concealing much. Always a sort of pathetic, and, at the same time, exultant strain rises, and is repeated as the changes go on; now we hear the faint tinkle—signal to those aloft on the "bridges" to open more glories. Now some of the banks begin to part slowly, showing realms of light with a few divine beings—fairies—rising slowly here and there. More breaks beyond, and more fairies rising with a pyramid of these ladies beginning to mount slowly in the centre. Thus it goes on, the lights streaming on full in every colour and from every quarter in the richest effulgence. In some of the more daring efforts the *femmes suspendues* seem to float in the air or rest on the frail support of sprays or branches of trees. While, finally, at the back of all the most glorious paradise of all will open, revealing the pure empyrean itself, and some fair spirit aloft in a cloud among the stars; the apex of all. Then all motion ceases; the work is complete; the fumes of crimson, red, and blue fire begin to rise at the wings; the music bursts into a crash of exultation; and, possibly to the general disenchantment, a burly man, in a black frock coat, steps out from the side and bows awkwardly. Then, to a shrill whistle, the first scene of the Harlequinade closes in, and shuts out the brilliant vision.

CHAPTER XVIII. PANTOMIMIC FAMILIES— GIUSEPPE GRIMALDI

—JAMES BYRNE, THE HARLEQUIN AND INVENTOR OF THE MODERN HARLEQUIN'S DRESS—JOSEPH GRIMALDI, JUNIOR—THE BOLOGNA FAMILY—TOM ELLAR—THE RIDGWAYS—THE BRADBURYS—THE MONTGOMERYS—- THE PAYNES—THE MARSHALLS—CHARLES AND RICHARD STILT—RICHARD FLEXMORE—TOM GRAY—THE PAULOS— DUBOIS—ARTHUR AND CHARLES LECLERQ—"JIMMY" BARNES—FAMOUS PANTALOONS—MISS FARREN—MRS. SIDDONS—COLUMBINES—NOTABLE ACTORS IN PANTOMIME.

In the histrionic profession the genius of hereditary is shown over and over again; and no more so than in Pantomimic families. For, if blessed with a numerous progeny, the sons became—the eldest, of course, could only, as the place of honour, be Clown—the others, Harlequins, Pantaloons; the daughters, Columbines; and, perhaps, Harlequinas.

In the last chapter but one I have referred to Grimaldi's father, Giuseppe Grimaldi, "Iron Legs," and now let us recall something more of the sire of so worthy a son.

As a dancer—as his father was before him—and Pantomimist, Giuseppe Grimaldi, before coming to England, had appeared at the fairs of France and Italy. In 1758 Giuseppe made his first appearance on the stage of Drury Lane, under Garrick's management, in a new Pantomime dance, entitled, "The Millers."

For some thirty years afterwards the Signor continued to be a member of the Drury Lane *corps de ballet*, and appearing as Clown, Harlequin, and Pantaloon.

In 1764, Giuseppe played Harlequin in a Clown-less Pantomime at Sadler's Wells, and in the Drury Lane Pantomime of the same year, though there were Harlequin, Pantaloon, and Columbine in it, there was no Clown. Drury Lane was then only open in the winter, and Sadler's Wells in the summer months.

A notable Harlequin was Mr. James Byrne, the ballet-master. "Mr. Byrne," says Grimaldi, in his "Memoirs," "was the best Harlequin on the boards, and never has been excelled, or even equalled, since that period."

Mr. Byrne came of a well-known dancing family, and to him we owe the introduction of the tight-fitting dress worn by Harlequin. Until the production of the Pantomime of "Harlequin Amulet, or the Magic of Mona," at Drury Lane Theatre, written by Mr. Powell, produced at Christmas, 1799, by Mr. Byrne, and which ran until Easter, 1800—it had been the loose jacket and trousers of the ancient Mimes. It had also been considered indispensable that Harlequin should be continually attitudinising in the five different positions of Admiration, Flirtation, Thought, Defiance, and Determination; and continually passing from one to the other without pausing. Byrne, for newer attitudes, abolished these postures, but long afterwards the old form of posing was, and is still, retained by the exponents of Harlequin.

In this Pantomime, Byrne, as Harlequin, appeared in a white silk close-fitting shape, fitting without a wrinkle, and into which the variegated colours of time-honoured memory were woven, and covered with spangles, presenting a very bright appearance.

Mr. Byrne, also gave the character of Harlequin an entirely new reading. The colours of Harlequin's dress had every one a significance, as follows:—Red, temper; blue, love; yellow, jealousy; brown or mauve, constancy. When Harlequin wore his mask down he was supposed to be invisible. On his mask he had two bumps, denoting knowledge on the one hand, and thought on the other, whilst in his cap he wore a hare's foot, and a worked device on his shoes, indicating flight and speed. Can we not from the bumps of knowledge and the hare's foot trace the characteristics of the god Mercury, which, as previously stated, was the prototype of Harlequin. With the bat, or magic sword, the gift from the fairies to him, Harlequin was supposed to be invulnerable, and if he lost his sword he would fall into the power of the Clown.

Byrne's innovation was not resisted, and it was well received, and ever since this memorable occasion, the character of Harlequin has, for the most part, been dressed as Byrne dressed it. The significance of the present-day variegated colours of Harlequin's costume are somewhat different to the above, and denote: red, fire; blue, water; yellow, air; and black, earth. These—the four elements—are typical of the regions governed by Mercury.

Mr. Byrne was at Drury Lane in the time of Garrick. He died December 4th, 1845, in the eighty-ninth year of his age. Mrs. Byrne, who was also a dancer, pre-deceasing her husband by a few months in her seventy-fourth year.

Joseph Grimaldi, son of "Old Joe," made, at twelve years of age, his first appearance at Sadler's Wells in 1814, playing Man Friday to his father's Robinson Crusoe. For several years both father and son played together in various Pantomimes; and it was thought that before young Joe there was a brilliant future. This, however, was soon dissipated, as he embarked upon vicious courses, and through a blow on the head received in some brawl "He became a wild and furious savage; he was frequently attacked with dreadful fits of epilepsy, and continually committed actions which nothing but insanity could prompt. In 1828 he had a decided attack of insanity, and was confined in a strait waistcoat in his father's house for some time."

From engagements at Drury Lane, Sadler's Wells, the Pavilion and the Surrey Theatre in turn, he was dismissed, finally "Falling into the lowest state of wretchedness and poverty. His dress had fallen to rags, his feet were thrust into two worn-out slippers, his face was pale with disease, and squalid with dirt and want, and he was steeped in degradation." This unhappy life came to a final close in a public-house in Pitt Street, off the Tottenham Court Road.

Signor Pietro Bologna, a country-man and friend of Giuseppe Grimaldi, Joe Grimaldi's father, brought with him from Genoa his wife, two sons and a daughter. They were all Mimes, and, in a Pantomime produced in 1795, entitled, "The Magic Feast," Signor Bologna was Clown, and his son, "Jack" Bologna, was Harlequin; the latter being also Harlequin to Grimaldi's Clown, both at Covent Garden and Sadler's Wells. "Jack" Bologna married a sister of Mary Bristow, Joe Grimaldi's second wife, and the mother of poor young Joe.

Tom Ellar was another famous Harlequin, first making his appearance at the Royalty, Goodman's Fields, in 1808. For several seasons he played Harlequin at Covent Garden.

Many years ago penny portraits of Mr. Ellar "In his favourite character of Harlequin," were published by a Mr. Skelt, or a Mr. Park, of Long Lane, Smithfield, and were the delight of those, who, if living now, are old and gray.

Tom Ellar died April 8, 1842, aged 62. Previous to his death he must have fallen upon evil days, as Thackeray, in 1840, wrote: "Tom, who comes bounding home from school, has the doctor's account in his trunk, and his father goes to sleep at the Pantomime to which he takes him. *Pater infelix*, you too, have laughed at Clown, and the magic wand of spangled Harlequin: what delightful enchantment did it wave round you in the golden days 'when George the Third was King?' But our Clown lies in his grave; and our Harlequin Ellar, prince of many of our enchanted islands, was he not at

Bow Street the other day, in his dirty, faded, tattered motley—seized as a law breaker for acting at a penny theatre, after having well nigh starved in the streets, where nobody would listen to his old guitar? No one gave a shilling to bless him: not one of us who owe him so much!"

Another Pantomime family were the Ridgways. Tom Ridgway was Clown under Madame Vestris's management at Covent Garden.

There have been several Bradburys since the time of Grimaldi's great rival, Robert Bradbury, died July 21, 1831, who wore on his person nine strong "pads," in order to go through some extraordinary feats.

The Montgomerys; the Paynes, Harry and Fred; nor should the name of "Old Billy" Payne be omitted. "Billy" Payne it was, it will be remembered, who, in 1833, helped, from the stage of Covent Garden, the dying Edmund Kean.

Then there were the Marshalls, Harry and Joseph; Charles and Richard Stilt; and a very original and amusing Clown, Richard Flexmore, died August 20, 1860, aged 36. Tom Gray, a famous Clown of Covent Garden, died January 28th, 1768, aged upwards of 100 years; the Paulo family of Pantomimists; Dubois, Arthur and Charles Leclerq, Walter Hilyard, and many, many others.

In the 'twenties and 'thirties a popular and famous Pantaloon was "Jimmy" Barnes, died September 28th, 1838. Barnes, in the summer of 1830, was engaged to play in an English company at Paris, but they had hardly commenced to perform when the Revolution of July broke out. Some years afterwards Barnes published in "Bentley's Miscellany," from his old original M.S., an amusing and illustrated account of his wanderings.

Amongst other Pantaloons there have been—Thomas Blanchard, died August 20, 1859, aged 72; William Lynch, died June 29, 1861, aged 78; R. Norman, died September 16, 1858, aged 70; George Tanner, died February 8, 1870; and Paulo, a member of Mr. Charles Kean's Company at the Princess's Theatre, had as Pantaloon appeared in many Pantomimes. It is a notable fact that a good number of our Mimes were long-livers.

Long before Miss Farren, afterwards Countess of Derby (died April 21, 1829), first charmed a London audience, we hear of her in 1772 at Wakefield in one of her first parts—if not her first—that of Columbine. She could both sing well and dance gracefully. One of the earliest "parts" that even the great Mrs. Siddons (that afterwards was), when a young girl, played, was in connection with Pantomime, as Combes remembered to have seen her "Standing by the side of her father's stage, and knocking a pair of snuffers against a candle-stick to imitate the sound of a wind-mill, during the representation of some Harlequinade."

In days gone by Madame Leclerq, Carlotta Leclerq, Charles Kean's Columbine in the seasons of 1850-1-2, E. Dennett, Emma Boleno, died October 18th, 1867, aged 35; Marie Charles, who died from an accident by fire, Pavilion Theatre, January 21, 1864, and others have won considerable fame in the part of Columbine.

Amongst those who have played Harlequin in days gone by, have been the elder Kean, and the well-known actor, Mr. Wilson Barrett, who, early in his career, played this part for an extra two shillings and sixpence "thrown in," to augment his then weekly salary of seventeen shillings and sixpence; whilst Sir Henry Irving tells us that he also has appeared in Pantomime, in the character of a wicked fairy, named Venoma, in days since past, for a small monetary emolument.

CHAPTER XIX. POPULAR PANTOMIME SUBJECTS—POOR PANTOMIME LIBRETTOS

—PANTOMIME SUBJECTS OF OUR PROGENITORS—THE VARIOUS VERSIONS OF "ALADDIN"—"THE BABES IN THE WOOD"—"BLUE BEARD"—"BEAUTY AND THE BEAST"— "CINDERELLA"—"DICK WHITTINGTON"—"THE HOUSE THAT JACK BUILT"—"JACK THE GIANT KILLER"—"JACK AND THE BEANSTALK"—"RED RIDING HOOD"—"THE SLEEPING BEAUTY IN THE WOOD"—UNLUCKY SUBJECTS—"ALI BABA AND THE FORTY THIEVES"—"THE FAIR ONE WITH GOLDEN LOCKS"—THE SOURCE OF "SINDBAD THE SAILOR" AND "ROBINSON CRUSOE."

It may be of interest in this History of Pantomime to note the origin of some of our most popular present day Pantomime subjects, besides showing many of our present day Pantomime libretto writers that in such well-known themes as "Aladdin," "Cinderella," and others, there is no need to cast their stories pretty much in the same groove, year after year, when by drawing on the fairy-lore of the East much that is new and original, for present-day English Pantomimes, is waiting the attention of their skill and ingenuity.

Though the stories of popular English Pantomimes are practically the same each year (why I do not know), yet, not content with this, in many of our large cities and towns we frequently see the same Pantomime title not only "billed" at one theatre, but perhaps at several others. This clashing and clashing year after year with one another's titles (I say nothing about the "plots," as these, in many instances, only consist of a half-penny worth of author to an intolerable deal of music-hall gag), cannot but, I have long been of opinion, adversely affect the box-office receipts, unless, of course, the Pantomime-goer makes a point of "doing the round," so to speak, which, however, is not generally the case.

As Pantomime writers in the early days there were Thomas Dibdin, son of Charles Dibdin, the writer of nautical ballads, Pocock and Sheridan. Dibdin was one of the best of Pantomime librettists, and from the years 1771 to 1841 his prolific pen, as a writer of Pantomimes, was never idle, as from it came some thirty-three Pantomimes, and all successes. Amongst other literary luminaries, in after years, as writers of Pantomime Extravaganzas, there were J.R. Planché, E.L. Blanchard, W. Brough, Mark Lemon, H.J. Byron, Wilton Jones, and John Francis McArdle.

History always repeats itself we know, and poor Pantomime books were not unknown as far back as half a century ago, as the subjoined parody on the "Burial of Sir John Moore," by the late Albert Smith plainly shows:—

Not a laugh was heard, not a topical joke,
  As its corse to oblivion we hurried;
Not a paper a word in its favour spoke

  On the Pantomime going to be buried.

We buried it after the Boxing Night,
  The folks from the galleries turning;
For 'twas plain it would scarcely pay for the light
  Of the star in the last act burning.

No useless play-bill put forth a puff,
  How splendid the public had found it,
But it lay like a piece that had been called "stuff,"
  With a very wet blanket around it.

After this digression for one brief moment more, let us take a passing glance at some of the Pantomime subjects which our progenitors delighted in. They had not the continual ringing of the changes on half-a-dozen Pantomime subjects, as we have at present, but revelled in such attractions as "Harlequin Don Quixote," "The Triumph of Mirth, or Harlequin's Wedding," "The Enchanted Wood or Harlequin's

Vagaries," "Hurly Burly, or the Fairy of the Wells," "Blue Beard, Black Beard, and Grey Beard," and many others. However, to return.

Of the Pantomime subjects, whose origin we are going to enquire into, let us first commence with "Aladdin."

According to the many versions of this popular story in Europe and Asia, it would seem that its origin originally was of Buddhist extraction. In our common English version of "Aladdin," in "The Arabian Nights," which was taken from Galland's French version, it is doubtless an Eastern picture. It does not occur, however, in any known Arabian text (says Mr. Clouston, in "Popular Tales," and to whose work I am indebted for much of the information for this chapter) of "The Thousand and One Nights" (*Elf Laila wa Laila*), although the chief incidents are found in many Asiatic fictions, and it had become orally current in Greece and Italy before it was published by Galland. A popular Italian version, which presents a close analogy to the familiar story of "Aladdin" (properly "*Alá-u-d-Din*," signifying "Exaltation of the Faith") is given by Miss M.H. Busk, in her "Folklore of Rome," under the title of "How Cajusse was married."

A good natured looking old man one day knocks at the door of a poor tailor out of work; his son, opening the door, is told by the old man that he is his uncle, and he gives him half a piastre to buy a good dinner. When the tailor comes home— he was absent at the time—he is surprised to hear the old man claim him as a brother, but finding him so rich he does not dispute the matter. After the old man had lived some time with the tailor and his family, literally defraying all the household expenses, he finds it necessary to depart, and with the tailor's consent takes the boy Cajusse with him, in order that he may learn some useful business. But no sooner do they get outside the town than he tells Cajusse that it is all a dodge. "I'm not your uncle," he says, "I want a strong, daring boy to do something I am too old to do. I'm a wizard—don't attempt to escape for you can't." Cajusse, not a bit frightened, asks him what it is he wants him to do; and the wizard raises a flat stone from the ground, and orders him to go down, and after he gets to the bottom of the cave to proceed until he comes to a beautiful garden, where he will see a fierce dog keeping watch. "Here's bread for him. Don't look back when you hear sounds behind you. On a shelf you will see an old lantern; take it down, and bring it to me." So saying the wizard gave Cajusse a ring, in case anything awkward should happen to him after he had got the lantern, when he had only to rub the ring, and wish for deliverance. Cajusse finds precious stones hanging like frost from the trees in the garden underground, and he fills his pocket with them. Returning to the entrance of the cave, he refuses to give up the lantern till he has been drawn out; so the wizard thinking merely to frighten him replaces the stone. Cajusse finding himself thus entrapped rubs the ring, when instantly the Slave of the Ring appears, and the youth at once orders the table to be laid for dinner. He then calls for his mother and father, and they all have an unusually good meal. Some time afterwards, Cajusse had returned home, the town was illuminated, one day in honour of the marriage of the Sultan's daughter to the Vizier's son. He sends his mother to the palace with a basket of jewels, and, to demand the Sultan's daughter in marriage. The Sultan is astounded at the purity of the gems, and says he will give his answer in a month. At the end of the same week the Grand Vizier's son is married to the Princess.

Cajusse rubs his lantern and says "Go to-night and take the daughter of the Sultan and lay her on a poor pallet in our outhouse." This is done, and Cajusse begins to talk to her, but she is far too frightened to answer. The Sultan learns of his daughter's whereabouts, and does not know what to make of the strange business. The son of the Vizier complains to his father that his wife disappears every night, and comes back just before dawn. Cajusse now sends his mother to the Sultan with three more baskets full of jewels, and the Sultan tells her he may come and see him at the palace. Having received this message, Cajusse rubs the lantern, gets a dress of gold and silver, a richly caparisoned horse, four pages with rich dresses to ride behind them, and one to go before, distributing money to the people. Cajusse is next married to the Princess, and they live together in a most magnificent palace with great happiness. By-and-bye the old wizard hears of this, and resolves to obtain the lantern by hook or by crook. Disguising himself as a pedlar he comes to the palace calling out the familiar "New lamps for old." By this means he obtains the precious lamp, and immediately transports the palace and the princess to an island in the high seas. Cajusse, by the aid of the magic ring, quickly follows, to find his princess a prisoner in the power of the wizard. He then gives her this advice: "Make a feast to-night; say you'll marry the old wizard if he'll tell you what thing would be fatal to him, and you will guard him against it." The princess gets from the magician the fatal secret. "One must go into a far distant forest," he says "Where there is a beast called the hydra, and cut off his seven heads. If the middle head is split open a leveret will jump out and run off. If the leveret is split open, a bird will fly out. If the bird is caught and opened, in its body is a precious stone, and should that be placed under my pillow I shall die." Cajusse accomplishes all these things, and gives the life-stone to the princess, together with a bottle of opium. The princess drugs the wizard's wine, and when he had laid his head on his pillow (under which was the stone) he gave three terrible yells, turned himself round three times, and was dead. After thus ridding themselves of their enemy, Cajusse and his bride lived happy ever afterwards.

Aladdin's adventure with the magician in the enchanted cave has also its counterpart in Germany (see Grimms' German Collection).

Another "Aladdin" version is the tale of Marúf, the last in the Búlák and Calcutta printed Arabic texts of the "Book of Marúf" in "The Thousand and One Nights." The story is to the effect that Marúf had given out that he was a rich man, under which false pretence he marries the Sultan's daughter. The tale he spread about was that he was expecting the arrival of a rich caravan, which contained all his princely wealth. After they were married, Marúf confesses to his wife the imposture he has practised on them. She urges him to fly, or his head would be forfeited, and procures him a disguise to flee the country. He does so, and, whilst journeying through a village, he sees a man ploughing in a field, whom he asks for food. Whilst the latter is away, Marúf continues the ploughing, where the man had left off, and the ploughshare strikes against something hard in the ground, which turns out to be an iron ring in a marble slab. He pulls at the ring, and Marúf discovers a small room covered with gold, emeralds, rubies, and other precious stones. He also discovers a coffer of crystal, having a little box, containing a diamond in its entirety. Desirous of knowing what the box further contains, he finds a plain gold ring, with strange talismanic characters engraved thereon. Placing the ring on his finger, he is suddenly confronted by the Genii of the Ring, who demands to know what are his commands. Marúf desires the Genii to transport all the treasure to the earth, when mules and servants appear, and carry it to the city which Marúf had left, much to the chagrin of the Vizier, who did not like Marúf. Marúf, during a great feast prepared for the occasion, tells the Sultan how he became possessed of the treasure, when the Sultan begs the loan of the ring, which Marúf hands to the Vizier to give him, and which no sooner does he get, than he commands the Genii to convey Marúf to some desert island, and leave him to die. The Vizier also serves the Sultan the same way, and then he turns his attention to "Mrs. Marúf," whom he threatens with death if she refuses to marry him. At a banquet she makes the Vizier drunk, obtains possession of the ring, secures the return of Marúf and the Sultan, and the decapitation of the Vizier.

The "Babes in the Wood" was registered on the books of Stationers' Hall as a ballad as far back as 1595.

To take another familiar Pantomime subject, "Blue Beard," this story is said to have been invented as a satire on our King Henry VIII. There is little doubt, however, of it originating from a very ancient source; and to afford the reader all the possible information on the subject, a writer in "The Drama," a magazine of the beginning of the last century has the following, though he does not state his authority for the information:—

As this extraordinary personage has long been the theme, not only of children's early study and terror, it will be gratifying to peruse the character of that being who really existed, and who was distinguished in horror and derision by the strange appellation of "Blue Beard."

He was the famous Gilles, Marquis de Laval, a Mareschal of France, and a General of uncommon intrepidity, who greatly distinguished himself in the reigns of Charles VI. and VII., by his courage, particularly against the English, when they invaded France. He rendered such services to his country, which were sufficient to immortalize his name, had he not for ever tarnished his glory by the most terrible and cruel murders, blasphemies, and licentiousness of every kind. His revenues were princely; but his prodigality was sufficient to render even an Emperor a bankrupt. Wherever he went he had in his suite a seraglio, a band of players, a company of musicians, a society of sorcerers and magicians, an almost incredible number of cooks, packs of dogs of various kinds, and above 200 led horses. Mezerai, an author of great repute, says, that he encouraged and maintained men who called themselves sorcerers, to discover hidden treasures, and corrupted young persons of both sexes to attach themselves to him, and afterwards killed them for the sake of their blood, which was requisite to form his charms and incantations. These horrid excesses may be believed, when we reflect on the age of ignorance and barbarism in which they were certainly too often practised. He was at length, for a state crime against the Duke of Brittany, sentenced to be burnt alive in a field at Nantz in 1440, but the Duke, who was present at his execution, so far mitigated the sentence, that he was first strangled, then burnt, and his ashes buried. Though he was descended from one of the most illustrious families in France, he declared, previous to his death, that all his terrible excesses were owing to his wretched education.

"Blue Beard" was first dramatised at Paris, in 1746, when "*Barbe Bleu*" was thus announced:—*Pantomime—representée par la troupe des Comediens Pantomimes, Foir St. Laurent.* It was afterwards dramatised at the Earl of Barrymore's Theatre, Wargrave, Berks., and in 1791. After that the subject was produced at Covent Garden Theatre as a Pantomime.

"Beauty and the Beast," the latter a white bear, is to be found in "Popular Tales from the Norse," by Mr. Dasent, and in the collection of "Popular Tales from the German" by the Brothers Grimm. As a ballad the story of "Beauty and the Beast" is a very old one.

"Cinderella" is to be found in the language of every European country. In ancient Hindu legends it appears; in tales related by the Greek poets it is also to be found.

The story of "Cinderella," according to the ancient Hindu legends, is that of the Sun and the Dawn. Cinderella has been likened to Aurora, the Spirit of the Dawn, and the fairy Prince of the legend is the morning Sun, ever closely pursuing her to make her his bride. The Hindu legend of the lost slipper is that a wealthy Rajah's beautiful daughter was born with a golden necklace, which contained her soul, and, if the necklace was taken off and worn by someone else, the Princess would die. The Rajah gave her on her birthday a pair of slippers with ornaments of gold and gems upon them. The princess went out upon a mountain to gather flowers, and whilst stooping there to pluck the flowers, one of her slippers fell into the forest below. A Prince, who was hunting, picked up the slipper, and was so charmed with it that he said he would make the wearer his wife. He made his wish known, but no one came to claim the slipper; at length word was given to the Prince where to find the Rajah's daughter; and shortly afterwards they were married. One of the wives of the Prince, being jealous of the Rajah's daughter, stole the necklace, put it on her own neck, and then the Rajah's daughter died. The Prince, afterwards, found out the secret of the necklace, and got it back again, and put it on his dead wife's neck, and she came to life, and they lived ever afterwards in the greatest harmony.

The ancient Grecian version of "Cinderella" is that of the story of a beautiful woman named Rhodope, who, whilst bathing, an eagle flew away with one of her slippers to Egypt, and dropped it in the lap of the King as he sat at Memphis on the judgment seat. The King was so attracted by the smallness and beauty of the slipper that he fell in love with the wearer, and afterwards made her his wife.

In Tuscany, Persia, Norway, Denmark, Russia, the story of "Dick Whittington" is well known. In all probability, like many other fairy tales, its origin was from a Buddhist source. The English version, that the Lord Mayor Whittington was the poor ill-used boy he is represented to have been in the popular tale seems quite impossible, since according to Stow (mentions Mr. Clouston) he was the son of Sir Richard Whittington, Knight. The story was current in Europe in the thirteenth century. In the chronicle of Albert, Abbot of the Convent of St. Mary of Slade, written at that period, it is related that there were two citizens of Venice, one of whom was rich, the other poor. It fortuned that the rich man went abroad to trade, and the poor man gave him as his venture two cats, the sale of which, as in our tale of the renowned "Dick Whittington," procured him great wealth.

On September 21st, 1668, Pepys makes mention in his diary of going to Southwark Fair, and of seeing the puppet show of "Whittington," which he says "was pretty to see." A

Pantomime on the subject was also given by Rich early in the eighteenth century.

In Tuscany, the "Dick Whittington" story runs that in the fifteenth century, a Genoese merchant, who presented two cats to the King, was rewarded by him with rich presents.

In Norway, a poor boy, having found a box full of silver money under a stone, emptied the box and its contents into a lake—one piece, however, floated, which he kept, believing it to be *good*. His mother, hearing of this, thrust him out of doors; and he eventually obtained employment in a merchant's house. The merchant, having to make a voyage to foreign parts, he asked each of his servants what he should "venture" for him. The poor boy offered all he had, the silver penny, of which he was still the possessor. With this the merchant purchased a cat, and sailed away, but the vessel in which he was in was driven out of her course on to the shores of a strange country. The merchant going ashore went to an inn, and, in a room, he saw the table laid for dinner, with a long rod for each man who sat at it. When the meat was set on the table, out swarmed thousands of mice, and each one who sat at the table beat them off with his rod. The cat was brought into service, and sold for a hundred dollars, and soon put an end to the career of the mice. When the merchant had weighed anchor, much to his surprise, he saw the cat sitting at the mast head. Again foul weather came on, and again the vessel was driven to another strange country, where the mice were just as numerous as before. The cat was called in, sold this time for two hundred dollars, and away the merchant sailed. No sooner, however, was he at sea, than the cat once more appeared before him. The vessel was again driven out of her course to another strange country, over-run with rats this time, when poor pussy was sold a third time, for the sum of three hundred dollars. Again the cat made its appearance; and the merchant thinking to do the poor boy out of his money, a dreadful storm arose, which only subsided on the merchant making a vow that the boy should have every penny. When he arrived home the merchant faithfully kept his promise, gave the boy the six hundred dollars, and the hand of his daughter besides.

A Breton legend of the story of "Dick Whittington" runs that three sons go to seek their fortune, the eldest of whom, Yvon, possesses a cat. The cat again plays an important part. Yvon becomes the friend of the Lord of the Manor, and has gold and diamonds bestowed upon him in galore.

The Russian version is that a poor little orphan boy buys a cat, which some mischievous boys were teasing, for three copecks (about a penny). Taken into the service of a merchant the latter goes to a distant country, accompanied by the cat of the orphan boy. Puss making sad work of some rats, which threatened to make an end of the merchant in the inn, which he occupied. He ultimately sold the cat to the landlord for a sack full of gold. Returning home, on his way thither, he thought how foolish it would be to give all the money to the boy. Whereupon a dreadful storm arose, and the vessel, in which was the merchant, was in danger of sinking. The merchant, knowing that the storm had arisen through his change of purpose, prayed to heaven for forgiveness, when the sea became calm, and the vessel arrived safely in port, when the merchant paid over to the orphan boy all the wealth obtained by the sale of the cat.

In the Persian version, unlike the other legends, the cat is owned by a poor widow, who had been impoverished through her sons, and was left with only a cat. The sale of the cat produces great wealth; and the widow, Kayser, immediately sends for her sons to share her newly-acquired fortune. What follows is different to the other versions of these wonderful cat stories. The sons only too eager to share the wealth of their mother, fit out many vessels, and begin to trade largely with India and Arabia. Thinking that to acquire wealth by commerce alone, rather slow work, they turned pirates, and were a source of trouble and annoyance to the neighbouring states, till about 1230 A.D., when they were reduced to vassalage under Persian rule.

"The House that Jack Built" has its prototype in a sacred hymn in the Talmud of the Hebrews.

"Jack, the Giant Killer" and "Jack and the Beanstalk" are two very ancient themes coming from the North, of the time, it is said, of King Arthur, and of the days when "Giants were upon the earth." The well-known cry of the giants in these legends—

"Fe, Fi, Fo, Fum,

I smell the blood of an Englishman;

Be he alive or be he dead,

I'll grind his bones to make my bread,"

is also referred to by Shakespeare in "King Lear," in Act III., Scene 5, when Edgar sings:—

"Child Rowland to the dark Tower came;

His word was still, fee, foh, and fum,

I smell the blood of an Englishman."

The English version of the story of "Jack the Giant Killer," must, therefore, be older than the time of Elizabeth. It is also a strange and significant fact that amongst the Zulus, and the inhabitants of the Fiji Islands, there are similar legends of the story of "Jack and the Beanstalk."

The story of "Jack and the Beanstalk" is also to be found in old Hindoo tales, in which the beans denote abundance. The Russians have a story in which a bean falls to the ground, and an old man, the Sun, climbs up by it to heaven. "The ogre in the land above the skies," observes Mr. Baring Gould, "who was once the all-father, possessed three treasures—a harp, which played of itself enchanting music; bags of gold and diamonds; and a hen which daily laid a golden egg. The harp is the wind, the bags of gold are the clouds dropping the sparkling rain, and the golden egg laid every day by the red hen is the producing sun." The same idea in "Jack and the Beanstalk" occurs in the fairy legends of the North and the East, as well as in Grecian stories.

In "Jack the Giant Killer," the gifts given to Jack are found in Tartar, Hindoo, Scandinavian, and German legends.

Now let us note briefly the origin of "Red Riding Hood" and "The Sleeping Beauty in the Wood." All the other fairy stories that we know of are to be found in other countries, and springing originally from Asia, where they were made ages and ages ago.

The Wolf in the story of "Red Riding Hood" has been likened to the days of our own "Bluff King Hal," owing to the latter's suppression of the monasteries, and Red Riding Hood herself, whom the Wolf subsequently eats, with her hood and habit, was supposed to be typical of the monastic orders.

The Hindoo's version of the "Red Riding Hood" story is a pretty and fanciful one. Their idea was that there was always a great Dragon endeavouring to devour Indra, the Sun god, and to prevent the Sun from shining upon the earth, Indra ultimately overcomes the Dragon. Red Riding Hood, with her warm habit, is supposed to be the setting sun casting its red and glittering rays as it sinks to rest. The old Grandmother is Mother Earth; and the Wolf, the Dragon; and when all is dark and still, the Wolf swallows the Grandmother, namely, the Earth; and afterwards, as Night has fallen, the Evening Sun. The Huntsman denotes the Morning Sun, and he chases away all the dark clouds gathered during the night, and by doing so kills the Wolf; recovers the old Grandmother Earth, and brings to life again, Little Red Riding Hood. Another version (observes Mr. T. Bunce) is that the Wolf is the dark, and dreary winter, that kills the Earth with frost, but when spring comes again it brings the Earth and the Sun back to life.

In "The Sleeping Beauty in the Wood," the maiden has been likened to the Morning dawn, and the young Prince, who awakens her, with a kiss, to the Sun.

"Ali Baba and the Forty Thieves," in concluding this chapter, I may say, with "The Fair One with Golden Locks," forms to the superstitious the only two unlucky Pantomime subjects.

"Sindbad, the Sailor," taken from the "Arabian Nights," has its origin in Persian and Arabian tales.

Of all our Pantomime subjects, "Robinson Crusoe," seems to be the only one we can properly lay claim to as being "of our own make," so to speak, and written by Daniel De Foe, and, in the main, from the imagination. De Foe, it has been stated, derived his idea for this story from the adventures of one, Alexander Selkirk, a Scotchman, who had been a castaway on the Island of Juan Fernandez. The first portion of "Robinson Crusoe" appeared in "The Family Instructor," in 1719, of which De Foe was the founder. It, at once, sprang into popularity, and has left its author undying fame. De Foe was born about 1660 in the parish of St. Giles, Cripplegate, died 26th April, 1731, and was buried in Bunhill Fields.

CHAPTER XX. PANTOMIME IN AMERICA.

Pantomime, in America, had not a very long run, it being killed by the farcical comedy. Mr. E.L. Blanchard supposes that "Mother Goose" was the first Pantomime played in America, but this is an error, as it was not until 1786, when Garrick's "Harlequin's Invasion," and R. Pocock's "Robinson Crusoe" were played at the John Street Theatre, New York, that Pantomime made its advent in America. "Mother Goose" was afterwards played, but it did not suit the Yankee's taste. Rich's Harlequin, Gay of "The Beggars Opera," produced at Lincoln's Inn Fields Theatre, and which it is said made "Rich Gay, and Gay Rich," also went to America, and where, it is said, he became the Chief of an Indian tribe in the Far West. In the South Sea Bubble Gay held some £20,000. His friends advised him to sell, but he dreamed of greatness and splendour, and refused their counsel. Ultimately, both the profit and the principal was lost, and Gay sunk under the calamity so low that his life became in danger.

American Pantomimes consisted of a semi-pastoral "opening," performed almost entirely in dumb show, and a big trick Harlequinade, and down to the time of Pantomime's decease in America was it played like this.

George L. Fox made Pantomime highly popular in America. Born in May of 1825, he, as an actor and comedian in Yankee and Irish parts, held his own in popularity with the great Joseph Jefferson.

Fox might be properly termed "The Grimaldi of America," as he was the representative Clown of the land of the stars and stripes. His Clown's parts he dressed like Grimaldi, and with the whitened face and bald head of Pierrot, the French type of Clown.

The year that "Mother Goose" came to New York saw the introduction of a French troupe of Pantomimists, known as the Ravels. In imitation of these performers Fox introduced in the 'fifties ballet Pantomimes, and several Ravelsque pieces like "The Red Gnome" and "The Schoolmaster" with good results.

In 1862 Fox was at the Bowery Theatre, and, during his occupation of the same, he did much to popularise Pantomime. Half a dozen years afterwards we find him at the Olympic Theatre, New York, where he produced "Humpty Dumpty," which ran 483 nights, and for five years, till 1873, it held its place, on and off, in the bill. Altogether it was played 943 times. Fox, from this, was known as Humpty Dumpty, and, strangely enough, also, the Americans for long enough afterwards called every Pantomime "Humpty Dumpty."

Fox was a very good mimic, imitating all the Hamlets of the day, besides being a good melodramatic actor. He died October 24th, 1877, at Cambridge, Mass., of softening of the brain.

Tony Denier, a pupil of the Ravels, and a quondam friend of Fox, next took Fox's place in the estimation of the American public. Of Denier, we are told that he arrived in Boston in 1852, with the proverbial half-crown in his pocket. He was of French extraction, and descended from one of the best French families. In 1863 he was with P.T. Barnum, and appearing as a one-legged dancer. In 1868, he went into Pantomime, toured "Humpty Dumpty," and for some twenty years afterwards kept the Pantomimic ball merrily rolling until his retirement at Chicago into private life. Denier made Harlequinade tricks a speciality.

Pantomime in America may be said to have lived about a quarter of a century; but in the autumn of this year (1901) Pantomime, as we now know it in this country, made its first appearance at the Broadway Theatre, New York, when last year's Drury Lane annual, "The Sleeping Beauty and the Beast," was successfully presented. It is very probable that this class of entertainment will become very popular in America.

CHAPTER XXI. PANTOMIMES MADE MORE ATTRACTIVE

—THE RESTRICTIVE POLICY OF THE PATENT HOUSES— "MOTHER GOOSE" AND "GEORGE BARNWELL" AT COVENT GARDEN—LIVELY AUDIENCES—"JANE SHORE"— "HARLEQUIN PAT AND HARLEQUIN BAT"—"THE FIRST SPEAKING OPENING"—EXTRAVAGENCE IN EXTRAVAGANZAS—THE DOOM OF THE OLD FORM OF PANTOMIME—ITS REVIVAL IN A NEW FORM—A PIECE OF PURE PANTOMIME—PRESENT DAY MIMETIC ART— "*L'ENFANT PRODIGUE*"—A RETROSPECT—THE OLD WITH THE NEW, AND CONCLUSION.

Pantomimes, as they grew, were made more and more attractive, "new scenery, decorations, and flyings" were introduced, and with new "flyings," of course, more accidents.

The restrictive policy adopted by the Patent theatres—till the repeal of their patents (1843)—towards the minor houses, which gave to the former the sole and only right of performing the "legitimate" was, by the minor theatres, infringed in many ways. The means adopted was the employment of Pantomime in the depiction of plays adapted and considered suitable for the minor theatres. These were entirely carried on by action, and when the actor could not express something that had to be explained, like the names of characters, a scroll, with the necessary details inscribed thereon, was unrolled in full view of the audience. These entertainments were very popular at the close of the eighteenth century, and they were also the means of providing some first-class Pantomimists—as, for instance, Bologna and D'Egville.

In a couple of volumes by Mr. J.C. Cross, entitled, "Circusiana," the author of many of these old "dumb shows," the reader can see what they were like. The scripts of these plays consisted, like our ancient "Platts" and the Italian Scenarios, of principally stage directions.

John Palmer, the actor who died on the stage of the Theatre Royal, Liverpool—now used for the purpose of a cold storage—after uttering, in the part of "The Stranger," the words "There is another and a better world," found that, after building his theatre, the Royalty, in Wellclose Square, that he was prohibited its use, used to give Pantomimic representations, and just in a similar way as what the minor theatres did, as mentioned above.

It is amusing to note how the titles of some of Shakespeare's works—which at one time the Patent theatres had the monopoly—were got over; "Hamlet" has been known to have been played as "Methinks I see my Father;" "Othello," as "Is He Jealous?;" "Romeo and Juliet," as "How to Die for Love;" "The Merchant of Venice," under "Diamond Cut Diamond," and so on. Music and dancing also were introduced *ad lib* into these performances.

The Pantomime of "Mother Goose," produced at Covent Garden, December 29, 1806, which ran 92 nights, was preceded by "George Barnwell," and brought some £20,000 into the theatre treasury. Strangely enough, for about thirty years, it was the unvarying rule to play "George Barnwell" at this theatre on a Boxing Night, which, from all accounts, owing to the liveliness of the gods and goddesses assembled on these occasions—the Tragedy was as much a Pantomime as the Pantomime proper that followed. Of these "merry moments" Dibdin recalls that Tragedies, Comedies, and Operas were doomed to suffer all the complicated combinations of "Pray ask that gentleman to sit down," "Take off your hat?" and the like. "But the moment," continues Dibdin, "the curtain goes up (on the Pantomime), if any unfortunate gentleman speaks a word they make no reply, *but throw him over directly.*"

Seemingly afterwards, at Pantomime time, "Barnwell" was discarded in favour of "Jane Shore," as in "The Theatrical Magazine" we find a writer penning the following:—

A few years since it was the established rule to play "George Barnwell," by way, we suppose, of a "great moral lesson" to the apprentices of London. In this age of innovation this venerable custom has been broken down, but the principle seems not wholly to have been abandoned. "Jane Shore" has supplanted "Barnwell," and the anxieties of the age, are, it would appear, now directed towards the softer sex. Seriously speaking, we consider these Christmas selections as exceedingly absurd. Visitants at this period of the year frequent the theatre less for the purpose of seeing the play than the Pantomime, and at both theatres it was this evening their chief, and almost only, attraction; for the tragedy of Rowe, which is of very little merit, derived but trifling interest or effect from the performers who personated the prominent characters. Moreover the lessons of the pulpit have unfortunately but too slight an influence on those who attend them, and we are rather fearful the moral benefits to be derived from these stage lectures, to the apprentices and servants of the metropolis, do not countervail the loss of pleasure sustained by those who would be so much better pleased; and, therefore, perhaps, taught by a lively comedy, satirising some of the light vices or laughable follies of the age. We trust this theatrical nuisance will be for the future reformed; we can almost excuse the holiday folks for being turbulent, when we reflect upon the insult offered to their understandings, in the treatment they receive on these occasions.

In 1830, at Covent Garden Theatre, Peake introduced into the Pantomime of "Harlequin Pat, and Harlequin Bat" a "speaking opening." Pantomime, however, pursued the even tenour of its way until the production at the Adelphi, about

1857, of a Pantomime, with a "burlesque opening," and "the thin end of the wedge" was provided, written by Mark Lemon. In the Harlequinade, Madame Celeste appeared as Harlequin *à la Watteau*, and Miss Mary Keeley was the Columbine. These Extravaganzas, from the pen of Planché, with scenery by Beverley, and all under the management of Vestris, afterwards became quite the rage.

I have previously referred to the excellence of Beverley's scenes under the *regime* of Madame Vestris. Extravagance in Extravaganzas, like "The Blue Bird," "Once Upon a Time," and the like, caused the managers, in the matter of scenery, to enter into serious competition with one another.

Pantomime, it was thought, was doomed, as its decease at this epoch seemed impending. It managed, however, to come again into popular favour, but in a very different shape. Instead of the usual comic Pantomime it was played by two different sets of performers, and having no connection with one another. The opening scenes, like a soap bubble, began to grow larger and larger, the double plot was abandoned, the Transformation scene became the principal feature, and a long Harlequinade at the *end*.

In the Pantomime of "Red Riding Hood," written by F.W. Green, and produced at Her Majesty's Theatre, during the 'eighties, an effort was made to compose and invent a piece of pure Pantomime. The Vokes family, J.T. Powers, and others, appeared in this Pantomime.

In France and Italy particularly, the Mimetic Art still flourishes; but in this country it is practically a lost Art. One of the best examples, and most successful, we have had in recent years of this ancient form of entertainment in this country was that of "*L'Enfant Prodigue*," played by Mdlle. Jane May and a French Company of Pantomimists. There are, however, several other very brilliant Pantomimists excellent in their Art, like the Martinetti troupe, the two brothers Renad, and the Leopolds.

"It is a pity (observes Dickens, in 'The Theatre') that the knowledge of it (Pantomime) cannot be more extended among our modern actors and actresses, so few of whom understand anything about the effectiveness of appropriate gesture. A few lessons in the business of Harlequin would teach many a young man, for instance, the simple lesson that arms may be moved with advantage from the shoulder as well as from the elbow; and so we should get rid of one of the awkwardest, ugliest, and commonest of modern stage tricks. And there would be nothing derogatory in the study. Many of our most distinguished actors have graduated in Pantomime."

Mr. Davenport Adams, writing in "The Theatre," for January, 1882, on the decline of Pantomime, says:—

"We may say of present-day Pantomime that the trail of the music-hall is over it all. I admit the extreme ability of certain music-hall comedians. I object, however, altogether, to the intrusion of such artists into the domain of Pantomime, and I do so because they, and others not so able, bring with them, so to speak, an atmosphere which it is sad to see imported into the theatre. They bring with them, not only their songs, which, when offensive in their wording, are sometimes made doubly dangerous by their tunefulness; not only their dances, which are usually vulgar, when they are not inane, but their style and manner and 'gags,' which are generally the most deplorable of all. The objection to music-hall artists on the stage is, not only that they take the bread out of the mouths of 'the profession,' which is a minor consideration for the public, but that they have the effect of familiarising general audiences, and children especially, with a style and a kind of singing, dancing, and 'business' which, however it may be relished by a certain class of the population, ought steadily to be confined to its original habitat. The managers are, of course, very much to blame, for it is by their permission, if not by their desire, that youthful ears are regaled with 'W'st, w'st, w'st,' and similar elegant compositions. Such songs as these would not be tolerated by *paterfamilias* in his drawing-room, yet, when he takes his children to the Pantomime, they are the most prominent portion of the entertainment."

In the last century, Pantomimes, in the form so dear to our forefathers, sometimes twice yearly—at Easter and Christmas—were given. The comic and other scenes were in that true sense of the word humorous and funny. The reason was not far to seek, as they were all played by *actors*. The music-hall had not, as far as Pantomime was concerned, made such inroads as at the present time it has done into the dramatic profession. Clown, to *pater* and *materfamilias*, and others, was a source of genuine enjoyment; and though they may have passed the sere and yellow leaf of age, the laughs and hearty merriment of their grand-children gathered around them made them think of other days, when they were young themselves. Picture them all, dear reader, sitting in the Family Circle—now termed the Dress Circle—a happy party with smiling and contented faces, laughing at some *genuine acting*—Pantomime though it be—no *double entendre* songs, and nothing to be ashamed of.

To the young a visit to the Pantomime was invariably a yearly occurrence to be joyfully remembered till the next Boxing Day came round again. Do they, or can they, understand Pantomime in its present form? I very much doubt it.

When towards the close of the 'fifties, and the double plot was abandoned, the character of Harlequin began to be played by women, the origin of what is now known as the "principal boy," and some acrobatic turns, or other speciality business, began to be introduced during the course of the Pantomime, which greatly discounted the efforts of Harlequin and Clown.

Another competitor that took up the running to the abolition of Clown and his companions, was the music-hall, which began introducing Pantomimes and ballets. The first to do this, some years ago, was the Canterbury, other halls soon following suit.

The managers of the theatres took up arms, with the result that various decisions, chiefly averse to the music-halls, were obtained. A decision of the Court of Common Pleas left the music-halls in a position to give ballets with costume and scenic effects without any such control or precautions as was exercised in theatres under the Lord Chamberlain's authority. The duration of the litigation was all owing to the vague definition "Stageplays in the 6 and 7 Vict. c. 68," and of "Music, dancing and public entertainments in the Act 25, Geo. II., c. 30."

Of present-day Pantomime, with the immense sums spent annually on its gorgeous spectacular display and costly dresses, there is no necessity for me here to dilate upon, as it is a subject that is well known to us all. All that is beautiful about it is due principally to the scenic artists and the costumiers. The best parts are, as a general rule, allotted to music-hall "stars," whose names will draw the most money. And the followers of Thespis have, until the reign of King Pantomime is over, to take oftentimes second-class places in the Pantomimic form of entertainment of the present day.

In the old days everyone looked forward to the performances of Clown and his companions; but little by little their business went, until finally this has dwindled down to about one or two scenes—which, in some few instances is still retained.

And now to formally "ring down," and in writing the "tag," there is, I may say, with the sound of the prompter's bell, a melancholy ring as the passing knell of Clown and his merry companions, and the "tag," as it were, their epitaph.

Pantomimes—as our forefathers knew them—have become a thing of the past, and the survivors, Clown and his comrades, the former whose quips and quiddities, in childhood's happy days, many of us still lovingly remember; the wonderment with which we gazed at the magical tricks wrought by Harlequin and his wand; the quaint conceits and ambling gait of Pantaloon; and, last but not least, bewitching Columbine, with whom, most likely as each year came round, in youthful ardour we fell anew in love's toils, are all rapidly vanishing into the dim and distant past, and to live in the future only in the memory.

CURTAIN.

www.ingramcontent.com/pod-product-compliance
Lightning Source LLC
Chambersburg PA
CBHW020002290326
41935CB00007B/277